# The Self-Love Compass for Teen Girls

## Simple Steps to Navigate Life's Challenges, Love Your Body, Crush Self-Doubt, and Embrace Your Uniqueness with Confidence



Miranda Nunez

THE
SELF-LOVE
COMPASS

ISBN 978-82-694352-1-4

Published by *The Self-Love Compass™*

www.theselflovecompass.com

hello@theselflovecompass.com

Editor: Renny van der Deen

This book is for informational and personal development purposes only. It is not intended to replace therapy, counseling, or medical advice. If you are experiencing mental health challenges or need additional support, please seek help from a qualified professional.

While every effort has been made to ensure the accuracy and usefulness of the content, the author and publisher make no guarantees about the outcomes or results of applying the material in this book.

Your self-love journey is deeply personal. What works for one person may not work the same for another. Take what resonates, leave what doesn't, and move at your own pace.

Parental discretion is advised for younger readers. Some topics may encourage reflection that benefits from adult support and open conversations.

*The Self-Love Compass™* and Miranda Nunez are not liable for any damages or outcomes resulting from the use or misuse of this material.

# Contents

To the girl I used to be:

the one who doubted her worth, questioned her voice,

and tried so hard to fit in.

This is for you.

And to every teen girl holding quiet questions in her heart,

wondering if she's enough:

You are.

May these pages remind you of your power,

your beauty, and your right to love yourself deeply.

You were never too much.

You were always more than enough.

# Introduction

You know that feeling, don't you? That nagging voice in your head that whispers, "You're not good enough," or "You don't fit in." It's a voice that seems to grow louder each year as the pressures of being a teen girl in today's world weigh heavily on your shoulders. Trust me; I've been there. I've stood in front of the mirror, scrutinizing every inch of my body, wishing I could change everything about myself. I've felt the sting of rejection, the fear of not measuring up, and the overwhelming desire to be accepted for who I am.

But here's the thing: You are not alone. A staggering seven out of ten girls believe they are not good enough or don't measure up in some way. That is a heartbreaking statistic. It is also a powerful reminder that we're all in this together. We're all navigating the ups and downs of being a teen girl, trying to find our place in a world that often feels like it's constantly judging us.

That's why I wrote this book. I wanted to create a transformative guide and compass to help you and every other teen girl out there embrace self-love, build unshakable confidence, and navigate life's challenges with grace and resilience. This book isn't just another self-help book filled with empty clichés and unrealistic advice. No, this is a compass explicitly designed for you, with practical strategies, relatable stories, and actionable steps you can start implementing in your life now.

I know firsthand how tough it can be to love yourself in a world and society that constantly tells you to change. As a teen girl myself, I struggled with body image issues, self-doubt, and the constant pressure to fit in. But through my journey of self-discovery and personal growth, I've learned that true self-love isn't about changing who you are; it's about embracing every part of yourself, flaws and all. I don't want you to be well in your twenties before you start your self-love journey like I did. I had to take the long route to get there because I didn't have a book like this to guide me. So, I wrote this book for you, the younger me, and the teen girl in our family who is currently struggling. I've got you, girl. You are not alone.

This book delves deeply into the key themes and topics most relevant to your life. We'll explore how to embrace your uniqueness, cultivate a positive self-image, practice creative self-care, navigate social influences, and develop the emotional resilience that'll carry you through even the most challenging times. Each chapter is designed to build upon the last, providing you with a comprehensive compass for self-love that you can refer back to again and again.

But this book isn't just about reading and absorbing information. It's about taking action. That's why I've included some opportunities to write, a quiz, and some exercises throughout the book that will help you apply the concepts to your own life. I want you to actively participate in your journey of self-discovery and growth because that's when the real magic happens. Please make sure to download your free mini-workbook by scanning the QR code at the end of this introduction. If you want a more comprehensive workbook, you can buy it at the same place you got this book. The comprehensive workbook includes all exercises in the mini-workbook. I want you to embark on this journey and feel the positive change. You can follow the comprehensive workbook while reading this book.

To keep you inspired and motivated, I've included uplifting quotes from strong female role models at the beginning of each chapter. These women have faced their challenges and triumphed, and their words of wisdom will serve as a small reminder that you, too, have the power to overcome anything that comes your way.

When you reach the end of the book, I hope you'll have gained a newfound sense of self-esteem, body positivity, and the confidence to embrace your individuality. You'll have a toolkit of practical strategies and insights that you can turn to whenever you need a little extra support or guidance. But most importantly, you'll have taken the first step on a lifelong journey of self-love and personal growth.

So, are you ready to embark on this transformative journey with me? Are you prepared to let go of self-doubt, embrace your uniqueness, and step into your power as the fantastic, one-of-a-kind young woman you are? If so, let's dive in together. Your journey to unshakable self-love starts now.

**Scan the QR code to receive your gift: a mini-workbook to follow this book**

SCAN ME

**OR: Scan the QR code to buy the comprehensive workbook here:**

SCAN ME

@THESELFLOVECOMPASS

Chapter One

# Embracing Your Unique Journey

"Don't try so hard to fit in, and certainly don't try so hard to be different. Just try hard to be you."

Zendaya

Have you ever felt like you're pretending to be someone else? Or like you were wearing a mask, hiding your true self from the world? Maybe it was at school, where it seems like your classmates have it all together. Or perhaps when you're scrolling through social media, comparing your life to photos of flawless people and their lives. It's easy to lose yourself trying to fit in, especially if you feel unsure of where you fit in or even belong. But here's the truth: You don't need to be like anyone else. You don't need to hide who you are. You don't need to prove your worth. Your journey is uniquely yours, and it's time to embrace that.

This chapter is about understanding what self-love truly means and how it can transform your life. It's about learning to love yourself without filters, masks, or excuses. It's an invitation to celebrate your individuality and recognize that you are enough just as you are. It's about seeing your uniqueness as a strength, not something to fix. And it's your first step toward building real self-love that lasts.

- You are not broken.
- You are not behind.
- You are not alone.
- You are enough, right now, just as you are.

## Understanding Self-Love: A Teen's Perspective

Self-love isn't just a trend or a hashtag. It's not a burst of confidence that comes and goes. It's an ongoing, steady relationship with yourself, rooted and built on self-acceptance, honesty, and respect. Think of it as the foundation supporting your happiness, confidence, and purpose. It's about embracing the parts of you that aren't perfect and realizing that they're what makes you real. Loving yourself is a bold, powerful choice in a world that constantly tells you to fit in. Self-love is a powerful rebellion against anyone or anything that makes you feel like you're not enough.

Self-love isn't the same as self-care. Self-care might mean taking time for a face mask, taking a long bath, or putting your phone away for the night, and that matters. But self-love goes deeper. It's about knowing who you are, listening to your emotions, and honoring your needs without shame. No judgment towards yourself. It's about creating a safe space inside yourself to grow, even when things feel complicated or messy. It allows you to learn from setbacks. This awareness leads to compassion, allowing you to be gentle with yourself, especially when you feel like you're falling apart or things don't go as planned.

When you choose self-love, you start seeing yourself in a different light. You begin making decisions that reflect your worth. You let go of people or habits that bring you down. You surround yourself with those who uplift and respect you. You speak up, set boundaries, say no when necessary, and take care of your mental and emotional health. You stop chasing perfection and start showing up for yourself, day by day, step by step. It's an ongoing process, not a destination.

This isn't about getting it all right. It's about showing up with love, even when things go wrong. Ask yourself, "What would Love do?" or "Is this loving to me?" Self-love is a practice, not a finish line. The journey is messy and beautiful. Every day gives you a new chance to grow into the person you already are underneath the doubt. And that person? She is more than enough.

## Debunking Myths About Self-Love

Let's clear up some of the biggest myths about self-love, because these false beliefs can make it feel confusing, out of reach, or even wrong to care about yourself.

One common misconception is that self-love is selfish. Maybe you've heard things like, "You're full of yourself," or "You should care more about others than yourself." I used to hear, "Focus on what you can do for others instead of spending so much time on yourself." However, self-love isn't about thinking you're better than anyone. It's about knowing who you are, honoring your true self, accepting your feelings, and showing kindness. As coach Christie Inge points out: "When you love yourself first, your capacity to love others expands."

Another myth is that self-love equals arrogance. This couldn't be further from the truth. Confidence and arrogance aren't the same. Arrogance is loud and often covers up insecurity. Real self-love is quiet. It's grounded in self-respect. You know your worth without needing to prove it or put anyone else down to feel good. Just like Amy Morin said: "Be the woman who fixes another woman's crown without telling the world it was crooked."

Take 15-year-old Kayla. For a long time, she thought loving herself meant being vain. This was what she saw and interpreted when she grew up. She was afraid people would think she was full of herself if she showed pride or confidence. Luckily, Kayla had an older sister in her twenties, Leah, who was learning to practice self-love, and she guided Kayla. Over time, Kayla realized that valuing herself didn't mean she had to seek attention or compare herself to others. It meant standing tall in who she was, unapologetically. That shift helped her support others as well because she wasn't busy tearing herself down anymore.

Self-love is also often confused with vanity. But it's not just about skincare routines, perfect selfies, or picking the *right* outfit. Sure, those things can be acts of care, but they're not the whole picture.

I remember Alyssa, a girl I went to school with. I think Facebook had only been live for about a year. Yeah, I know, I'm *that* old. Anyways, back to the story. Alyssa wouldn't leave the house without perfect makeup and always posted polished photos on social media. On the outside, it looked like she had it all together. But inside, she was constantly comparing herself, chasing likes, and second-guessing everything. Over time, Alyssa realized she didn't have to earn her worth through her appearance. Self-love, for her, became about feeling okay in sweatpants, being honest about bad days, and appreciating the way she lifted her friends or made people laugh.

These stories show something important: Self-love isn't a destination. It's practice. And the more you let go of the myths, the more room you create to build a kind, steady relationship with yourself.

## The Science Behind Loving Yourself

Think of your mind like a garden. Each thought and feeling you have is a seed. Some grow into flowers: kindness, confidence, hope. Others turn into weeds: self-doubt, fear, stress. When you understand the science of self-love, you learn how to take care of that garden. You know how to help good stuff grow.

Let's start with a well-known psychological idea: Maslow's Hierarchy of Needs. It shows a pyramid with different layers; at the bottom of the pyramid is the layer of your basic needs, like food, safety, and connection. At the top of the pyramid is something called *self-actualization*, and to reach this, each previous layer of needs needs to be met. That's where self-love really begins to bloom. It's the place where you stop just surviving and start thriving.

Research from Dr. Kristin Neff adds something powerful to this. She studies self-compassion, treating yourself with the same kindness you'd give a friend. Her studies show that being kind to yourself makes you emotionally stronger. You bounce back faster after setbacks. It's not just about feeling good. It's about being able to handle life when things get hard.

Even your brain changes when you love yourself. Self-love helps your brain release chemicals like dopamine and serotonin, your natural "feel-good" messengers. These chemicals boost your mood, reduce stress, help you focus, and support your immune system. These processes are all part of neuroplasticity, which means your brain can grow and change based on your thoughts. How crazy is that? When you practice positive self-talk, you're actually rewiring your brain to be calmer, clearer, and more focused, making it easier to feel more relaxed during tests, exams, or stressful social situations. Just being loving towards yourself can make a big difference in your daily life.

Take 14-year-old Jasmine. She used to freeze up before tests, telling herself she wasn't smart enough. The more she believed that, the harder it became to concentrate on studying. Her mom noticed, and together, they started practicing self-love. Jasmine reminded herself that mistakes didn't define her, and she and her mother slowly noticed a change. Jasmine felt calmer. She focused better. And even when she didn't get the perfect grades, she kept showing up for herself without all the pressure and fear.

When you believe in yourself, you're more likely to try, to keep going, and to learn from your mistakes. That's what makes the real difference: not perfection, but persistence. Both academically and socially, self-love makes you stronger. It helps when you speak up when something feels wrong. It gives you the confidence to walk away from drama or peer pressure. It's not that you're suddenly a genius, but by regarding yourself more positively, you're more likely to succeed in school. This is because you're more motivated and less afraid of making mistakes. As mentioned before, you don't need to prove your worth to anyone when you know your worth.

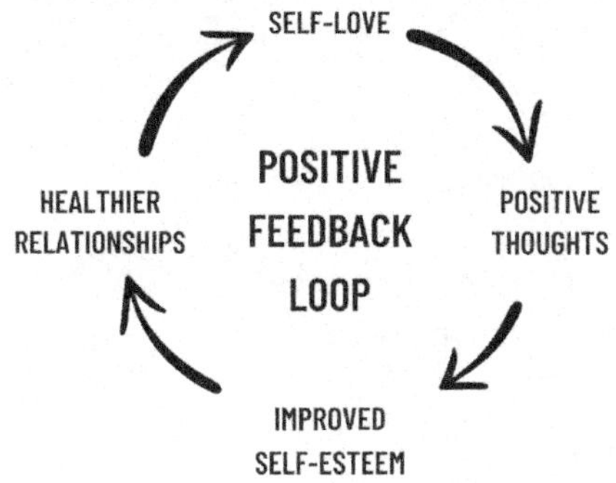


And here's the big picture: the self-love you build now shapes the rest of your life. It leads to stronger relationships, more confidence, and a steady sense of who you are, no matter what life throws your way.

## The Power of Personal Narratives: Your Story Matters

Think of your life as a book. Each chapter, each moment, shapes who you are. These stories aren't just memories. They form the way you see yourself. They tell you where you've been and show you where you're going.

Storytelling has helped people pass down culture, tradition, and wisdom for centuries. Through stories, we connect with the past, make sense of the present, and dream about the future. Your story is part of that tradition. It matters to you and the people around you.

When you honor your story, you validate your experience. You say, "My life has value." And you show others that it's okay to be different, struggle, and grow. That kind of honesty inspires more honesty. And that creates a real connection.

Take 13-year-old Nia. She's a first-generation daughter of immigrants and used to feel out of place when classmates talked about vacations or family traditions she couldn't relate to. She kept quiet, thinking her story didn't matter. But when she wrote about her experience with a school project, something shifted. Her classmates listened. Her teacher thanked her for sharing. And for the first time, Nia saw her story not as something to hide but as something to be proud of. Something that was uniquely hers.

Your story has that same power.

We grow and learn when we hear stories from people with different backgrounds. We become more understanding. More open. That's why diversity matters. It helps us build empathy, challenge assumptions, and find beauty in differences.

Your identity comprises many layers: culture, race, gender, beliefs, values, and life experiences. This is called *intersectionality*. It means your story can't be summed up by just one thing. You're not one label. You're a mix of experiences that create something entirely unique. And that uniqueness? That's your strength.

As activist Zainab Salbi said, "Leadership is about encouraging women to break their silence and tell their stories to the world." When you share your truth, you permit others to do the same. You create a ripple effect of courage and confidence. That's how change begins. So don't hold your story back. Own it. Honor it. And let it remind you and others that every journey matters.

## Celebrating What Makes You, You

When everyone seems to be chasing the same trends, it's easy to forget what makes you stand out. But what are your unique traits? They're not flaws. They're your superpowers. Maybe you're the one who makes your friends laugh until their stomachs hurt. Perhaps you love solving puzzles or helping people feel seen. These things matter. They're a part of who you are.

To recognize your strengths, try making a personal strength inventory. Write down everything you like about yourself, big or small. This isn't bragging. It's about acknowledging what you bring into the world. It could be your creativity, sense of humor, patience, or loyalty. Every strength counts.

Your values are just as important. These beliefs shape your decisions and guide how you treat yourself and others. Knowing what you stand for helps you stay grounded, even when life is confusing.

Amara, a 16-year-old, values honesty. She's known for speaking her truth, even when it's not the easy thing to do. Her friends trust her because they know she's real with them. When she shares her opinion, people listen. Not because she's loud but because she's clear, respectful, and consistent. That's the power of living by your values. You become someone others respect and someone you respect, too.

Take time to list your core values. What matters to you? What do you want to stand for? The more you connect with those answers, the stronger your sense of self becomes.

Another part of owning who you are is resisting the pressure to blend in. Society often tries to define what's "normal" or "cool," but those rules don't have to apply to you. Maybe your fashion style doesn't match what others wear. Maybe your interests are different from those of your peers. That's okay. Being yourself is more freeing than trying to fit a mold. When you express who you are–through your words, style, and passions–you inspire others to do the same. You show them that being authentic is brave and that standing out can be something to celebrate, not hide. So keep showing up as *you* because no one else can do it better.

## Opportunity to write:

1. What do people come to you for, even if you don't always notice it yourself? (Pay attention to what others trust you with. It might reveal a strength you overlook.)

2. When was the last time you surprised yourself in a good way? (Think of a moment you handled something better than expected. What did it show you about your strength?)

3. What's one thing about you that's quiet but powerful? (Your loudest traits aren't always your strongest. Look closer.)

4. What would you never trade, even if it made life easier? (This might be one of your core values.)

5. Who's someone you admire–and what do they stand for? (What you respect in others often reflects what matters most to you.)

6. When have you felt most proud of your decision, even if it was hard? (That moment likely lined up with one of your values.)

## Celebrating Cultural and Personal Heritage: Owning Your Identity

Your cultural heritage is part of your story. It comprises traditions, languages, beliefs, and values passed down through generations. It gives you a sense of belonging. It helps you understand who you are and where you come from. Think of your heritage as a mirror. It reflects your family's way of celebrating holidays, telling stories, sharing meals, and honoring traditions. These pieces of your life, big or small, are threads in the fabric of your identity.

It can feel exciting and confusing for teens growing up with more than one culture. You might feel like you're moving between worlds. But each culture you carry adds richness, depth, and perspective. Your identity isn't one thing. It's a blend that's uniquely yours.

Leila, a 15-year-old, has a Mexican mother and a Lebanese father. She used to feel unsure of where she fit in. She was too Latina in one group and not "Middle Eastern enough" in another. But as she grew older, she began leaning into both sides of her heritage. She learned traditional recipes from her grandma, practiced Arabic calligraphy with her dad, and started journaling about her experience as a bicultural teen. What once felt like a tug of war became something powerful: a celebration of *all* of who she is.

Engaging with your heritage can be a joyful and healing experience. Try cooking a dish your family has made for generations. Dance to music your parents grew up with. Ask a grandparent or relative about what life was like for them growing up. These moments connect you to something bigger than yourself. They remind you that you're part of a legacy and that legacy lives on through you.

But honoring your culture isn't always easy. You might feel pressure to choose between your heritage and your personal goals. You might feel *different* when your background isn't fully seen or understood. You might face stereotypes or questions that make you uncomfortable. These experiences might take some strength to face.

Loving where you come from is a form of self-love. You also have the power to help others feel seen. When you speak up about your experiences, support diverse friendships, or share your traditions, you create space for others to do the same.

Look at communities where people from all cultures unite, not to erase differences but to celebrate them. That's the world you help create when you own your identity and make space for others to do the same. Your story matters. Your roots matter. And by celebrating your heritage, you grow stronger in who you are and help others be themselves as well.

## Embracing Imperfection: The Beauty of Being Flawed

Trying to be perfect in every part of life–school, friendships, hobbies–can feel like a full-time job. And honestly? It's exhausting. Perfection might seem like the goal, but it often leads to stress, anxiety, and never feeling good enough. Instead of chasing flawlessness, focus on progress. Set goals that are realistic, not impossible. Celebrate small wins. Every step forward is a success, even if it's not perfect.

Perfectionism can become a loop that's hard to break out of. It tells you that whatever you do still isn't enough. That voice in your head grows louder when something goes wrong. You start fearing mistakes, so you avoid new things altogether.

I used to have that "do it perfectly or don't do it at all" mindset. Every time something didn't work out, that inner critic got nastier. Eventually, I stopped trying. Not because I didn't care, but because I didn't want to hear that voice anymore. But here's the truth: mistakes aren't failures. They're proof that you're trying, learning, and growing.

14-year-old Talia used to put intense pressure on herself to get straight A's. She panicked over every test and stayed up late rewriting assignments she'd already finished. It left her tired and anxious. One day, she broke down after getting a grade lower than expected. She had a long talk with her grandfather. He reminded her that getting those A's wasn't the be-all end-all. So, instead of giving up, she decided to try something new: being kind to herself. She started journaling after tough days, writing things like, "I did my best today" or "It's okay to learn from this." Over time, her stress eased, and she began to enjoy school again. Not because she was perfect, but because she allowed herself to be human.

Practicing self-compassion means being your own friend. It means forgiving yourself, trying again, and not letting one mistake define you. Tools like mindfulness, affirmations, and journaling help you stay grounded when that inner critic appears.

Perfection isn't what makes you lovable. Imperfections are what make you *real.* They help others connect with you. They remind you that growth isn't about getting everything right. It's about showing up, flaws and all, and loving yourself through it. So, let go of the need to be perfect. You don't need it to be enough. You already are.

## Crafting Your Personal Self-Love Definition

Remember the garden we talked about earlier in this chapter? Yeah, *that* garden. The one where self-love comes from planting and caring for something that grows over time. It might've sounded kind of cheesy, but stick with me. Self-love is like a garden you have to tend. Not because you're trying to be perfect, but because things can't grow without care. It's not about getting all the love or attention. It's about making sure your roots are strong so you have the energy and heart to show up for others. When you take care of yourself, you're not being selfish. You're laying the foundation for empathy, connection, and genuine kindness.

It starts with intention. Ask yourself: *Am I doing this because I care about myself? Is this choice helping me grow or am I feeling insecure?* Being honest with yourself keeps your version of self-love real and not just something that looks good on the outside.

Creating a personal self-love mantra is one way to ground yourself in that intention. A mantra is a short phrase that reminds you who you are and what you stand for. It can become your anchor in moments of doubt. Something like, "I am worthy of love and respect, just as I am," or "My imperfections make me unique and beautiful." Pick something that speaks to you. Say it while looking at yourself in the mirror. Write it in your journal. Use it when that inner critic starts getting loud.

And don't worry; your mantra can change. So can your definition of self-love. What worked for you last month might not work now. That doesn't mean you're doing anything wrong. It just means you're growing. Maybe meditation helps you today, but you might need something different later, like going for a nature walk or engaging in a creative hobby. The important thing is staying in tune with yourself and being open to adjusting when needed.

Self-love isn't one-size-fits-all. It's personal. It evolves with you. And when you craft your version, one that is rooted in honesty, care, and flexibility, you can genuinely rely on it.

## Opportunity to write:

1. If you could say one thing to your past self on a tough day, what would it be? (That message might be the start of your mantra.)

2. What words do you wish you believed about yourself, but aren't sure you do yet? (Turn those words into something you can grow into.)

3. What do you need to hear on the days when you forget how far you've come? (That reminder might be precisely what you need to move forward.)

## Let others' stories inspire you.

Stories you've read in this chapter and other stories you will read throughout the book are here to inspire you. They are more than just moments. They're reminders that growth is messy, brave, and possible.

When you hear stories from people your age, you don't have to copy them. You take the parts that resonate, the elements that speak to you, and carry those with you. Maybe it's someone's honesty, creativity, or how they stood up for themselves. Whatever it is, those small sparks can light the way in your own life.

Self-love doesn't grow in isolation. It is shaped by shared experiences, your struggles, your wins, and the support you give and receive along the way. The stories in this book are so powerful because they show that self-love doesn't look the same for everyone. It's influenced by where you come from, what you've been through, and what matters to you. That diversity is what makes each story meaningful.

And even though your journey is your own, you're not walking alone. Let these stories remind you of something: You're not the only one who's ever felt unsure, afraid, or different. You're also not the only one with strength, courage, and something important to say. Your story matters. Let it grow, allow it to guide you, and help others as a result along the way.

## The Self-Love Quiz: How's Your Inner Garden Growing?

Earlier in the chapter, I mentioned Dr. Kristin Neff, a leading researcher on self-compassion. She created the Self-Compassion Scale (SCS), which helps people understand how kind they are to themselves. She designed it for ages 14 and up.

Her work inspired me to create a shorter version just for this book, so you can get a sense of where you are on your own self-love journey.

## Take a Pause and Check In

Self-love is like a garden. It needs attention, care, and a little sunlight every day. This quiz helps you notice what your inner garden looks like right now, so you can understand what it needs to grow even stronger.

Be honest with yourself. This quiz isn't about getting the "right" answers. It's about checking in with where you are so you can keep moving forward with kindness and care.

**How to take the quiz:**
Read each statement and choose the answer that feels most true for you. Note or write down your answers.

**Answer options: A. Rarely B. Sometimes C. Often D. Almost always**

**Scoring - Give yourself: 1 point for every A 2 points for every B**

**3 points for every C 4 points for every D**

**Questions:**

**1- I speak kindly to myself, even when I make mistakes.**

**2- I know I have value, even when I feel unsure or down.**

**3- I make time to care for myself, like resting, saying no, or doing something I enjoy.**

**4- I accept the parts of me that feel messy, different, or that are still growing.**

**5- I stand up for myself when something doesn't feel right.**

**6- I let myself feel my emotions without judging or hiding them.**

**7- I celebrate the things I like about myself, both inside and out.**

**8- I don't compare my journey to others. I know I'm growing at my own pace.**

**9- I trust myself to make choices that are right for me.**

**10- I believe I'm worthy of love, just as I am today.**

**11- I forgive myself when I mess up instead of holding it against myself.**

**12- I feel at home with who I am, even while I'm still learning and changing.**

**Add up your total score.**

## What Your Score Says About Your Inner Garden

### 12-23 points – Nurturing Stage: You're planting the seeds

You're learning to care for yourself, even if it feels new or uncertain. You might still deal with harsh thoughts or question your worth, but just like a garden, this stage is all about starting fresh. With a bit of care, your self-love will begin to take root.

**Try this:**

- Speak to yourself the way you'd speak to a friend.
- Write one kind sentence about yourself each day.
- Choose one small act of self-care and follow through with it.

### 24-35 points – Blossoming Stage: You're starting to grow

You're beginning to believe in your values and treat yourself more kindly. Some days feel easier than others–and that's okay. It's part of the process. You're making choices that reflect your growth. Keep going. You're growing beautifully.

**Try this:**

- Notice your inner voice–soften it when it gets harsh.
- Set one boundary this week that protects your peace of mind.
- Do something creative, fun, or just for you.

**36-48 points – Radiant Stage: You're glowing from within**

You treat yourself with compassion, trust your worth, and show up for yourself with intention. You're growing from the inside out–and it shows. You'll always keep growing, but your self-love is strong and rooted. You're your own light.

**Try this:**

- Continue to be honest and gentle with yourself.
- Celebrate small wins–they matter.
- Share your light, but remember: you are your own sun.

No matter where you are, your self-love journey is valid and beautiful. Like any garden, it grows with care, patience, and attention. Be kind to yourself as you water what matters, pull the weeds, and reach for the sun. You don't have to rush. You're already growing in the right direction.

Once you've read more of this book and tried some tools and tips that speak to you, return to this quiz. See how your inner garden has evolved, and celebrate how far you've come.

CHAPTER TWO

# Embracing Your Body

"I finally realized that owning up
to your vulnerabilities is a form of strength."

Lizzo

## Your Worth Can't Be Edited

The following might sound familiar: You're scrolling through your social media feed, and all you see are flawless faces, toned bodies, glowing skin, and lives that seem effortlessly perfect. Everything looks curated, as if those people woke up in a magazine. It's easy to fall into the trap of comparing yourself. You wonder, "*Why don't I look like that?*" or "*What am I doing wrong?*"

This chapter is about those moments. The ones that make you question your reflection. The ones that chip away at your confidence. It's time to see social media for what it is and start embracing *yourself* for who you are.

Apps like Instagram and TikTok are filled with images that look real but often aren't. Between filters, lightning tricks, angles, and photo editing, what you see is usually a polished version of reality, if not a total illusion. Studies show that this kind of constant exposure can lead to body dissatisfaction, especially during the teen years when you're still figuring out how you feel about yourself.

If you've ever looked at a post and felt worse about yourself, you're not alone. And you're not imagining it. That feeling comes from comparing yourself to something that isn't real. Thankfully, more people are speaking up about it. Influencers like Mik Zazon and Sarah Nicole Landry are using their platforms to share unedited photos. They post their stretch marks, their body rolls, their acne, their scars. Their everyday body. And in doing so, they're breaking the illusion of perfection. They're saying, "This is what real looks like." And this message matters.

Real beauty isn't about flawless skin or perfect proportions. It's about honesty and confidence. Being comfortable in your skin, even when it's not filtered using a phone app. Photoshopped images can mess with your self-esteem. They create a standard you were never *meant* to meet. They show the highlight reel, not the real life behind it.

But once you understand this, you can look at those images differently. You can scroll and think; *good lighting, cool filters, but that's not real life.* And more importantly, you can stop letting those images define how you feel about yourself. Your worth isn't based on a filter or a like count. It's based on who you are, your kindness, laughter, strength, and energy. And none of those things need editing.

## Reflection Exercise: Unfiltered Reality

Let's pause for a second. Look at your social media feed. Are the accounts you follow lifting you or bringing you down? Start by choosing a few creators who make you feel seen, inspired, and good about yourself. Then, gently mute or unfollow anyone whose posts make you question your worth, even if they don't mean to. It's not about judging those people. It's about protecting your peace.

Now, grab a notebook or your notes app, and write down three things you love about your body. Not about things you *wish* were different. Not about things a filter could highlight. Just real, unfiltered you. Maybe it's your strong legs that carry you through the day, or that your eyes light up when you laugh. Or your hands that create, comfort, or hold the people you love. Whatever comes to mind, just write it down. Then keep that list somewhere you'll see it often. Let it remind you: Your body is already worthy. No edits are needed.

## Celebrating Your Body's Strength and Abilities

Imagine waking and feeling grateful for your body just as it is. That's the heart of body positivity. It's not about reaching a specific size or fitting into a mold. It's about respecting and appreciating your body for everything it does, regardless of shape, size, or ability. Body positivity teaches us to see beauty in diversity. To recognize that all bodies are worthy of love. And shift our focus from how our bodies *look* to what they *do.*

Think about it: your body carries you through every moment. It helps you breathe, move, speak, laugh, stretch, and rest. It does this whether you're tall, short, thin, or curvy. Whether you're dancing in your room, swimming with friends, or finishing a tough workout, those are moments of strength. Moments where your body shows up for you. Instead of criticizing how it looks, try celebrating what it can do. That's where absolute confidence starts.

Have you ever felt proud after a long hike or a swim? That rush of energy? That sense of "I did it"? Those feelings come from honoring your body's abilities, not its shape. Being part of body-positive spaces can help, too. Join a sports team. Attend a movement class that welcomes all sizes. Surround yourself with friends who uplift you, not because of your appearance but because of who you are.

Body acceptance leads to better choices, not out of shame but love. You start listening to your body. You rest when you need to. You nourish it because you care, not because you're trying to change it. Your body will change over time, and that's completely normal. Embrace it.

Think of athletes with disabilities who've redefined what strength means. They break records, challenge expectations, and inspire others by showing up fully in their bodies. Imagine a fashion designer creating clothes for all sizes, proving that style and self-expression belong to *everyone.* Their stories remind us that our bodies aren't limitations. They are possibilities.

So take a moment. Think about one thing your body did for you today. One thing you're proud of. Let that be enough. You don't need to look different to be worthy. You already are.

## Mirror Work: Seeing Yourself with Compassion

Standing in front of a mirror can feel uncomfortable, as if you're staring at someone you barely recognize. But mirror work isn't about judging your reflection. It's about learning to see yourself with compassion. Instead of focusing on flaws, this practice invites you to speak with kindness, to talk to yourself like someone you care about. It's not about vanity. It's about healing how you see yourself, one word at a time.

When you look in the mirror often enough, saying, "I am worthy of love and respect," or "I am proud of who I am becoming," something powerful happens. You start to shift your inner voice. You begin to believe the words you're saying. That's what mirror work does. It replaces harsh self-talk with uplifting affirmations. Over time, those words don't just sound nice; they start to feel true.

To begin, choose a time each day that works for you. Maybe it's the first thing in the morning or right before bed. Create a quiet space where you won't be interrupted. If it helps, play calming music or light a candle, whatever makes you feel safe and present. Then, look into your own eyes. This is where it starts. Speak your affirmations out loud, even if it feels weird, even if your voice shakes.

When I started mirror work, I didn't know what to expect. Sometimes, I laughed because I didn't believe the words. Other times, I cried because I finally *did.* Both reactions were real. And both were okay. So, give yourself grace if you feel awkward, emotional, or unsure. There is no wrong way to begin. Just showing up is enough.

To deepen the practice, try keeping a journal nearby. After each mirror session, write down what you felt or noticed. What affirmations came easily? Which ones felt hard to say? Over time, your journal becomes a reflection of your growth. A reminder of how far you've come. And a space to keep building a gentler, kinder relationship with yourself.

Mirror work is simple but powerful. It shifts how you see yourself in the mirror. And more importantly, it transforms how you show up in the world because you show up differently for yourself. Give it a chance, and see how you change.

## Fashion as Self-Expression: Dressing for You

Think about your favorite outfit. Maybe it's that cozy sweater you reach for on chilly mornings. Or those jeans that fit just right and make you feel like *yourself*. Fashion isn't just about what you wear. It's a form of self-expression. It's how you tell the world who you are without saying a word.

Your wardrobe is like a canvas. Each piece you choose is a brushstroke, reflecting your personality, mood, and individuality. That's the beauty of fashion: it gives you the freedom to show up for yourself in your own way, on your own terms.

And when you dress for *you*, not for trends, not for approval, it's an act of self-love. It's about choosing clothes that make you feel good and that feel *right* to wear. Clothes that let you breathe, move, and *be* in a way that feels natural. That kind of freedom is powerful. It gives you space to explore, experiment, and discover what makes you feel confident. Try different styles: boho, edgy, classic, sporty, soft, or bold. Fashion has no limits. You get to decide what fits you, inside and out.

I remember being so afraid to stand out. As a teen, I mainly wore gray. It felt safe, quiet, invisible. I used to love color as a kid, but somehow, along the way, I started hiding. One day, my best friend (she still is!) saw a new dress I bought and said, "Shocker. You got that beautiful dress in gray." She wasn't being mean. She just *knew* me. And her comment made me pause. Why did I always reach for the same shades? Since then, I've started leaning into colors that speak to me. Midnight blue, pine green, dusty blue, and dusty pink. Sometimes, even something teen-me would have called flashy. I still wear black and gray, but now it's a choice, not a shield.

That's what fashion should be: something that feels *you*. Start by noticing what makes you feel good. What pieces bring out your confidence? What colors or textures make you feel calm, strong, or bold? Your wardrobe is yours to create. Mix and match. Layer. Play. There are no rules, only possibilities.

Fashion isn't about fitting in. It's about self-discovery and empowerment. It's about showing up. It's about feeling like the best version of yourself, whatever that looks like today. So wear what feels like *you*. Not to impress, nor to hide. Celebrate your unique style. Just *shine* in your own way.

## The Comparison Trap vs. Constructive Comparisons

You're at a party, looking around the room. Someone's making everyone laugh. Another person looks flawless in their outfit. Someone else seems effortlessly confident. And then it hits you. *Why don't I feel like that? Why can't I be more like them?* That's the comparison trap. It sneaks in quietly but hits hard. Suddenly, you're questioning your worth, doubting your strengths, and forgetting everything that makes you *you*.

Comparing yourself to others is like running a race with no finish line. You just keep going, exhausted, frustrated, never feeling enough. It steals your joy. It clouds your confidence. And it makes it harder to see your beauty, growth, and progress. Comparison often starts with a trigger. Maybe it's a classmate who always gets top grades. Or someone whose life looks perfect on social media. It might be someone with similar goals to yours, and they get there before you. The trick is to notice *when* you start comparing and *why*. Understanding your triggers gives you the power to respond, not just react. Research shows that constant comparison can lead to anxiety and depression. It keeps you focused on what you *lack* instead of what you already *have*.

But here's the good news: You can shift this. Start by practicing **self-compassion**. When that inner critic pipes up, answer it with kindness. Try saying, "I am proud of how I listen deeply, or "I am doing my best, and that matters." Then, write it down. Keep a journal of small wins. Have you finished an assignment you were dreading? Write it down. Helped a friend through something challenging? Write it down. Celebrate those wins.

The more you focus on your milestones, the less noise other people's voices make. Turn comparison into curiosity, not envy. What do you admire in others? Is it their confidence? Their creativity? Instead of feeling less-than, let that admiration inspire you to grow.

And here's something to remember: Don't compare your *chapter 3* with someone else's *chapter 13*. You don't know the whole story. Some chapters are messy. Some are quiet. Some are breakthroughs in disguise. Focus on your chapter. Your growth. Your pace.

Set personal milestones and choose things that matter to *you*. Maybe you want to master a new hobby, improve your mindset, or build stronger boundaries. Whatever it is, track your progress against where *you* started. Because that's what growth is really about.

When you look at your past self and say, "Wow, I've come a long way," that's the only comparison that matters. You're doing better than you think. Stay focused on your journey. You've got this.

## Healthy Body, Healthy Mind: Finding Joy in Physical Activity

Imagine waking up refreshed, calm, and ready to take on the day. Your mind feels clear. Your energy feels steady. This happens when you care for your body, and your body takes care of your mind.

Physical activity isn't just about routines or results. It's a way to celebrate what your body can do. It boosts your mood, lowers stress, and lifts your self-esteem. When you move your body, you release endorphins. Those are "feel-good" chemicals that give you energy and help you manage stress. Even something as simple as a brisk walk, a short stretch session, or dancing in your room can shift your whole mood. It's a reminder that your body and mind are connected. Support one, and the other gets stronger too.

But the movement is just one piece. Fuel matters, too. What you eat affects how you feel. Nutritious, balanced meals give your brain the power to focus, think clearly, and manage emotions more easily. Starting your day with something nourishing, like a protein-packed breakfast or fresh fruit, can help you feel energized, focused, and steady all day.

It's not about eating perfectly. It's about giving your body the support it needs to help you feel your best. And here's something important to remember: Physical activity should feel *good*. It should bring you joy, not pressure.

Explore what movements feel fun and natural to you. Yoga, hiking, roller skating, dance workouts, team sports, bike rides, jumping rope, there are many ways to move. It doesn't have to be intense. It just has to feel good. You can also balance movement with stillness. Meditations, deep breathing, and quiet movements help your mind recharge. These practices build focus and calm, and pair beautifully with physical activity. Together, they help you stay grounded and strong.

And don't forget to rest. Resting isn't the same as being lazy. It's essential. Your body repairs, restores, and grows during rest. That's when the real magic happens. By moving your body, nourishing it with care, and allowing it to rest, you build a foundation for lasting well-being. Your body is your home. It's not something to punish or push. It‘s something to care for, celebrate, and appreciate daily.

As we wrap up this chapter, remember: You don't have to be perfect to be healthy. You just have to stay connected to what feels good, honest, and true for *you*. In the next chapter, we'll explore how to crush self-doubt and build confidence from the inside out.

Chapter Three

# Crushing Self-Doubt

"I'm not the next Usain Bolt or Michael Phelps.
I'm the first Simone Biles."

Simone Biles

## Quieting the Inner Critic

Have you ever experienced sitting in class and the teacher calls on you? Suddenly, your mind goes blank. And then that voice shows up. "You're going to mess up." "Everyone's watching." "You're not smart enough for this." That voice? That's your inner critic. It's the one that doubts you, questions your worth, and chips away at your confidence. You might hear it when you try something new, look at a photo of yourself, or step out of your comfort zone. It can be quiet and sneaky or loud and obvious. But either way, it feels personal, and it hurts.

Here's the thing: We all have an inner critic, even the people who seem the most confident. Understanding where that voice comes from is the first step to turning it down. Often, the inner critic is shaped by outside pressure: expectations from school, social media, or even your desire to fit in. Being shown images of perfect grades, perfect bodies, perfect lives. And when you don't match that image, the critic gets louder. But this isn't about absolute perfection. And that voice? It doesn't define you.

To quiet it, you need to start noticing when it shows up. Over time, you'll start to spot patterns. Perhaps the critic arrives before the tests. Or when you're around certain people. Or when you compare yourself to others online. Once you recognize the pattern, you can prepare for it and respond with kindness instead of criticism.

Another important step is paying attention to your self-talk. Are you telling yourself things like, *"I always mess up"* or *"I'll never be good at this"*? That kind of language reinforces the belief that you're not enough, which isn't true. When you catch yourself thinking like that, pause. Ask: *Is this thought helpful or harmful? Is it loving to me?* Instead of *"I'm so bad at this,"* try: *"I didn't do as well as I hoped, but I can learn from it and try again."* That's not fake positivity; it's honest, and it moves you forward.

There is a big difference between constructive and destructive criticism. **Constructive** feedback is specific. It helps you grow. "I didn't prepare enough for this presentation, so next time, I'll plan better." **Destructive** criticism is vague and cruel. It shuts you down. "I'm just terrible at public speaking." One helps you improve. The other one keeps you stuck. When you learn to tell the difference, your inner voice starts to shift from tearing you down to building you up.

Because here's the truth: You're allowed to make mistakes. You're allowed to grow at your own pace. You're allowed to speak to yourself with love. And that inner critic? It doesn't get the final say.

## Exercise: Thought Journal

One of the best tools for understanding your inner critic is a thought journal. Each day, take a few minutes to write down any negative thoughts you've had. What triggered it? What were you doing? How did it make you feel? Maybe it was a grade, a photo, or just something you said to yourself without even realizing it. After a while, go back and review your entries.

Do certain situations come up again and again? Are there specific people, environments, or emotions that bring out that critical voice?

This awareness gives you power. Because once you spot the patterns, you can begin to challenge them. You start to reframe those harsh thoughts into something more true and way more kind. Use whatever works for you: a notebook, a notes app, or a journaling app you like. The key is consistency. Make it part of your daily routine. Even writing a few sentences a day can help you grow more mindful and self-aware. This practice isn't about being perfect. It's about noticing and learning. And slowly, steadily turning the volume down on that voice in your head that says you're not enough.

And you're not alone in this. So many of us have faced that inner critic. And we've learned, with time and practice, how to respond with compassion instead of judgment. Every time you pause and reframe a thought, you're building a stronger foundation for self-worth. I want to share something personal with you. Once, when I first began working on a project, I was utterly overwhelmed. I'd hear my inner critic criticizing me for even trying to quiet her. Seriously.

One moment stands out. I had gotten some feedback on this project, which I had worked really hard on. I was talking to one of my best friends and said, "I hate that my *first* thought was 'I suck.' I hate that after all this work on believing I am enough, my first instinct is still *that.*" But later, I said, "Actually, I want to acknowledge something. Fifteen minutes after having that first thought, I remembered the truth: the mistakes mentioned in the feedback didn't mean I sucked. They didn't mean I had to quit. They were just things to improve. That feedback didn't define me. What mattered was how I was going to handle it. These mistakes wouldn't shape my future or ruin who I was. It was okay, I would learn from it."

And that hit me. A year earlier, I wouldn't have responded that way. I would've spiraled down and believed every word of that inner critic. But this time? I caught it. And I talked myself through it with honesty and care. That moment mattered. I felt sad that it took so long to get there. But also, I am so grateful that I *got there,* and that's what I want for you. You're on your journey. But if this book helps you in any way–even the smallest amount–I'm already thankful. Learning to quiet that inner critic doesn't happen all at once. It happens in moments. And those moments add up.

## Reframing Negative Self-Talk

Imagine waking up and immediately thinking, *"I can't face today."* It's just one sentence, but it sets the tone for everything that follows. Negative self-talk is sneaky. It creeps in quietly, while you're getting dressed, taking a test, or scrolling through social media. It can sound like: *"I'm so stupid," "I'll never be good at this," or "Nobody likes me."* If those thoughts go unchecked, they start playing on repeat like a sad song stuck in your head. The first step in changing that tune? Realizing it's there and choosing to switch to a different radio station. These thoughts often come from past experiences or social pressure that made you feel like you had to be "enough" to be accepted. But the thoughts are not who you are as a person.

Recognizing the pattern is where real change begins. Once you know how your mind is talking to you, it's time to reframe. Cognitive reframing involves rephrasing negative thoughts into more helpful and accurate ones. Try adding one simple word: yet.

"I can't do this" becomes "I can't do this... yet." See how that changes everything? "I failed" becomes "I will try again." "I'm bad at math" becomes "I'm learning how to be better at math." Small changes. Big shift. Ask yourself: *"Is this thought based on fact or fear? Is it helping me or holding me back?"*

Start responding with the same care you'd give to a friend. Because self-compassion matters. If your friend were struggling, you wouldn't say, "Wow, you're terrible at this." You'd say, "You're trying. I'm proud of you. You've got this." So why not speak to yourself in that way, too?

Here's one idea: write a letter to yourself. Yes, a real one. Tell yourself what you need to hear. Acknowledge what's hard. And remind yourself of everything you're doing right. Try something like: *"Today was tough, but I'm proud of how hard I tried. I am learning, and I'll keep showing up. I am resilient. I am growing."* Keep that letter somewhere safe. Read it when your self-esteem starts to wobble, and let it anchor you in the truth.

Another tool? Affirmations. Start collecting short, simple phrases that lift you. When a harsh thought sneaks in, replace it with something better. "I'm not good enough" is replaced with "I am enough, just as I am." "I'll never get there" is replaced with "I'm learning and growing every day." These words matter. And when you repeat them often, they start to feel more natural. More believable. More *you*.

Pair affirmations with mindfulness. When you notice negative self-talk coming up, take a deep breath. Inhale. Exhale. Let your thoughts settle like ripples on a calm lake. You don't need to fight the thoughts. Just notice them. Question them. And let them pass. Ask yourself: *"Why am I feeling this way?" "What's a more helpful way to see this?" "What can I learn from this?"* That's where the shift begins.

15-year-old Avery used to tell herself, "I'm not athletic." Every gym class made her feel small. She dreaded being picked for teams and felt embarrassed trying new activities. But one day, she decided to try something different. She started saying, *"I'm learning to enjoy movement."* She signed up for a beginner yoga class. She started slow and stuck with it. Over time, she realized that her old belief wasn't a fact. It was just a story she had been repeating. By reframing her thoughts, Avery found something she enjoyed and started feeling proud of what her body could do. She chose to rewrite her beliefs.

You can, too. The way you talk to yourself shapes how you see yourself. With a bit of practice, you can turn your inner voice into one that supports you rather than tears you down. You are not your worst thoughts. You are your resilience, your growth, your truth. And you have the power to rewrite the script.

## Embracing Vulnerability: Strength in Sharing Your Truth

Picture this: you're standing on the edge of a stage, about to share a piece of your heart. Your palms are sweaty, and your heart is racing. This is called *vulnerability*. It's raw. It's real. And yes, it's brave. Vulnerability is often misunderstood as weakness. But the truth? It takes strength to be seen. To speak up. To let someone in. Being vulnerable doesn't mean oversharing or exposing every part of yourself. It means being honest about what you're feeling, especially when it's hard. It means showing up as your authentic self without a mask.

Vulnerability is how we connect. It's how we grow. It's where trust begins. When you open up to someone you trust, you create space for a deeper connection. These moments, where you share something real, can change everything. Think about the people in your life who've shown you kindness and support. The ones who've listened, sat with you through challenging moments, or simply said, "I get it." Those are your safe spaces. That's where vulnerability thrives.

To start embracing vulnerability, build your inner circle by surrounding yourself with people who value honesty, not perfection. Practice active listening by giving your full attention when others share with you. When you lead with empathy, others will feel safe doing the same.

Let go of the need to be approved. Vulnerability isn't about getting permission to feel. It's about being true to who you are. Remember a time when you were honest about your feelings? Perhaps you confided in a friend about how hurt you were. Perhaps you admitted fearing uncertainty. And maybe, from that moment, something shifted. You felt lighter, stronger, more seen.

Those are moments worth reflecting on. Write about them. Meditate on them. Ask yourself: *What did I learn about myself? How did that moment change me?* These small reflections are signs of your courage and proof that you're growing.

Let quotes or stories guide you, too. Brené Brown once said, "Vulnerability is not winning or losing; it's having the courage to show up and be seen when we have no control over the outcome." That courage lives in you. And every time you choose to show up with honesty, whether it's with a friend, a teacher, a family member, or yourself, you build a life rooted in trust and genuine connection.

Vulnerability isn't a one-time thing. It's a practice. A mindset. A strength. And through it, you build emotional resilience, stronger relationships, and a more authentic life. So, as we close this chapter, ask yourself: *What truth do I need to speak? Who can I safely share it with?* You don't have to do it perfectly. You just have to show up. In the next chapter, we'll explore how social media shapes your self-image and how to take your power back.

# Chapter Four

# Navigating Social Media

"The greatest skill about having a platform, I think, is handing over the mic."

Yara Shahidi

## Your Feed, Your Power

Think about a time when you've just posted a photo on Instagram. The likes roll in, and with every one of them, there's a little rush. It feels good. But then the notifications slow down. And that high? It fades fast. Suddenly, you're wondering if the post was good enough. If *you* are good enough.

Welcome to social media, where likes, comments, and shares have become a form of "social currency." This currency can feel like it defines your value. The more "currency" you get, the better you feel. At least you will for a moment. But when it stops flowing in your direction, that's when the doubts start creeping in.

The dopamine effect of likes and comments is real. It creates a cycle where validation feels external, as if your worth depends on your audience. When the audience doesn't respond the way you hoped, it can leave you feeling anxious, unsure, or invisible. That's why creating a *curated digital space* is so important. Think of your feed like a room you spend time in every day. Would you fill it with voices that make you feel small? Or with people who uplift, inspire, educate, and reflect who you are? You get to choose.

Start by following accounts that make you feel good instead of wanting to be perfect. Look for creators who are honest, inclusive, and positive, and who understand you. Unfollow or mute anyone who makes you feel worth less than others. Even if they didn't mean to, even if everyone else follows them, you have the right to protect your peace. Your feed should reflect your *values*, not your fears.

To stay grounded, set boundaries. Limit your screen time. Try a weekly social media detox. Take breaks and reconnect with real life–your hobbies, your friends, and your thoughts. Sometimes, the most powerful thing you can do is log off. When you return, come back with intention. And come back with *critical thinking*.

Ask yourself: *Is this post real, or has it been filtered for perfection? Does this inspire me or make me feel like I'm falling behind? Is this someone's highlight reel or their whole story?* You don't have to stop being inspired by others. But don't let inspiration become pressure.

Follow creators who challenge toxic beauty standards. People who say, "You are enough as you are." Let their voices remind you that real is better than perfect. Try this: Scroll your feed. Pick a post that hits hard. Pause and ask: *What is this trying to tell me? Is it honest? Or is it selling me something, an image, a product, a standard I don't have to meet?*

That awareness? It's everything. The more intentional you become, the more control you take back. You stop letting your feed define you and start shaping it to reflect *who you are.* Because your worth is never in the likes; it's in how you live, how you show up, and how you treat yourself when the screen goes dark.

## Influencers vs. Real Life: Understanding Online Realities

It's hard to imagine a world without influencers, right? They're everywhere– on our feeds, in our explore pages, shaping trends and setting standards. From makeup tutorials to "a day in the life"-vlogs, influencers often feel like friends giving advice. That's part of what makes them so popular. They're relatable and accessible, and they let us into their lives, at least, the parts they choose to show. But even though they share snippets of their day, their struggles, and their triumphs, it's easy to forget this: Most of what we see is curated and carefully edited. Designed to inspire or sell.

That highlight reel? It's not the whole story. Some filters smooth out skin, and other tools reshape bodies. There are lighting tricks, edits, and brand partnerships–all working behind the scenes. It doesn't make them fake. It just makes them human. And understanding this is key to protecting your self-image.

Many influencers partner with brands and are paid to promote their products. That's their job. However, it also means that what they post might not be entirely personal; it might be strategic. It's okay to enjoy their content as long as you remember it's not always as spontaneous or authentic as it seems. It may be difficult to distinguish between genuine recommendations and paid advertisements. So, how do you tell what's real and what's not? It starts with being honest about how certain content makes you feel.

If you're scrolling and something consistently leaves you feeling like you're not enough, it's time to make a change. Do a social media audit. Go through the accounts you follow. Ask yourself: *Does this make me feel good? Seen? Encouraged? Or does it make me feel small?* If it's the latter, unfollow or mute the account. Not because you judge that person, but because you respect yourself. Follow people who uplift you. People who talk about real life, not just about the polished parts. Those who show up with creativity, honesty, and heart. People who reflect your values and inspire you to grow without making you feel like you need to change who you are.

There are influencers who champion self-love, body positivity, mental health, or empowerment. They discuss both struggles and wins. They remind you that imperfections are normal and that they don't make you less beautiful or less worthy. Those are the voices worth keeping.

The truth is, you don't have to post all the time or share your entire life to have a healthy relationship with social media. Honestly? I stopped posting a long time ago. I'm a private person, and I like sharing things with the people close to me, not the whole world. But I *do* still enjoy my feed. It's filled with what I love. Cute Yorkies (I have one), uplifting quotes for women, book content, and people talking about energy, goals, and growth. It's my space, and it reflects who I am and what inspires me. I stopped watching content that made me feel like I wasn't enough. Now, I scroll intentionally. I look for what aligns with *me*.

You can do the same. Your feed should reflect your real life, not someone else's highlight reel. It should remind you of your worth, not make you question it. You get to choose what you let in. That choice is your power.

## Authentic and Positive Online Presence: Being Real in a Virtual World

In a world full of filters, edits, and highlight reels, being your authentic self online is a bold and powerful choice. Think of your social media as a personal gallery. Each post, comment, and story is a piece of art that reflects your values, interests, and personality. It tells people not just what you *do* but who you *are*.

Begin by establishing a mission for your online presence. Something like, *"I want to share positivity and creativity and connect with others through honest storytelling."* Let that mission guide your choices. Consider what you post, share, follow, and the kind of space you want to create.

Choose platforms that match your vibe. Love photography? Try Instagram. Prefer sharing quick thoughts or casual updates? Snapchat is great for staying connected with close friends through everyday moments. Into short videos, storytelling, or creative edits? TikTok is perfect for self-expression, humor, and real-life content that feels relatable. Want space for deep writing or reflection? A blog might be your thing. Whatever you choose, let it reflect the real *you*, not what you think people want to see.

Authenticity builds connection. When you're honest about your thoughts, your struggles, and your triumphs, people feel it. They trust it. And they're more likely to be truthful in return. It's not always easy. Putting your authentic self out there can feel scary. But it's also how to build real communities.

14-year-old Liana started posting short captions about her experience with anxiety. Just a few thoughts about how she was feeling and what helped her get through tough days. She didn't expect much. But soon, other teens began responding. They said, "I feel this too," or "Thank you for saying this out loud." Her honesty made others feel seen. And it gave Liana the courage to keep showing up as herself. She shared her coping strategies, setbacks, and small victories. Over time, her online space evolved from just a profile to become a source of comfort and connection. That's the power of being real.

Being authentic doesn't mean you have to share everything. It means aligning your online self with your *real-life* values. It means treating others with kindness, even behind the scenes. It means speaking up when it matters and being quiet when you think it's wiser to do so.

Of course, being real online can come with fear of judgment. Not everyone will get you. And yes, some might be unkind. When that happens, take a breath before responding. Ask: *Is this helpful or just noise?* If it's not constructive, let it go. Not every comment deserves a response. Turn to the people who know you, the friends who remind you of your worth. They'll help you stay grounded in your truth. Because the more authentic you are, the more your people will find you. And the people who truly matter? They'll love you for exactly who you are, not for who you pretend to be.

Being real in a virtual world takes courage. But it also creates space for connection, confidence, and change. Let your voice reflect your truth. Let your presence inspire others to be themselves, too, because your authenticity is your superpower.

## Digital Detox: The Art of Unplugging

Close your eyes for a second and imagine a day when your phone isn't buzzing. There are no constant notifications. There is no pressure to post, just space. For your mind to breathe, your thoughts to slow down, and for you to be fully present. Taking a break from social media, even for a short time, can do more for your mental health than you might expect. A digital detox helps you reset, clear your head, and reconnect with what matters.

Research shows that being constantly plugged in can lead to increased anxiety, comparison, and self-doubt. Over time, that constant exposure can make you question your own life, even when nothing is wrong. Stepping away gives you room to come back to yourself. It creates space for calm, clarity, and self-awareness.

You might not always recognize when it's time for a break. But there are signs. Maybe you feel drained after scrolling, anxious when you're offline, or overwhelmed by the constant flood of information. Perhaps you catch yourself comparing everything you do to what others are posting. These are all signals. Your mind and body are telling you it's time to pause and protect your peace.

That doesn't mean you have to give up social media altogether. It's about balance and boundaries. You can start small. Set screen-free hours or schedule a day each week to unplug. Use that time to do something you enjoy without documenting it. Go for a walk, try painting, bake something, listen to music, or spend time with people in person. You can also set specific goals, such as reducing your daily screen time or introducing tech-free routines, like keeping your phone out of your bedroom or turning off notifications before bedtime.

16-year-old Hannah noticed she was checking her phone constantly. First thing in the morning, between every class, even while hanging out with friends. She felt anxious when she wasn't online. So she made a change. She turned off her notifications, moved her social media apps to a folder she couldn't see right away, and started checking in only once a day. At first, it felt uncomfortable. But after a few days, she began sleeping better, felt more focused, and realized she wasn't missing anything important. Now, she feels lighter, less anxious, and more in control of her time.

Turning off notifications has helped me a lot, too. I still check social media, but when I choose to. It's not because my phone is buzzing. Sometimes, I forget to check for days. And the truth is, it doesn't matter. Everyone important to me has my number. If something matters, they can reach me directly. That shift lowered my anxiety more than I ever expected. I don't feel the same pressure always to be available or constantly keep up. I've learned that social media is not everything. Letting go of the need always to be online gave me room to breathe.

Taking a break from the digital world isn't about disconnecting completely. It's about reconnecting with yourself, with your values, and with what brings you peace. It's about noticing how you feel, listening to what you need, and honoring it. This awareness is part of your self-love journey. It's a way to protect your energy and show up for yourself in real life, not just online. As you continue exploring what self-love means to you, remember that unplugging can sometimes be one of the most powerful ways to reconnect with your true self.

CHAPTER FIVE

# Building Authentic Relationships

"Friendships between women, as any woman will tell you, are built of a thousand small kindnesses... swirls of shared experience and gentle nudges of encouragement."
Michelle Obama

Have you ever found yourself sitting with a group of friends, laughter filling the air, each of you feeling safe and valued? A moment like this captures the heart of true friendship, a steady presence in the sometimes stormy world of growing up. Real friendships are built on trust, respect, and mutual understanding. They make room for your authentic self, with no pretending required. These relationships let you feel seen and supported, even when life feels uncertain. You don't have to be perfect to be loved. You just have to be you.

Friendships like these can help you grow. They give you courage. They lift you when you doubt yourself and help you feel grounded when the world feels heavy. But not every friendship offers that kind of support. Instead of helping you feel strong, some relationships will start to make you feel small. Over time, they chip away at your confidence. These are toxic friendships, and they are harder to spot than you might think.

Sometimes, it's not apparent right away. You may feel drained after hanging out with someone. Maybe someone said things that feel like "jokes" but leave you feeling hurt or insecure. Or perhaps people only show up when it benefits them, but disappear when you need support. If you find yourself feeling anxious, criticized, or like you have to shrink to stay in the friendship, these are signs that it might not be healthy. Words and actions that don't match, constant judgment, or a lack of empathy are serious red flags.

One way to sort through these feelings is to create a list of pros and cons. How do you feel after being with this person? Do they uplift you, or do they leave you second-guessing yourself? If someone constantly makes you feel like you have to change who you are to keep their approval, it may be time to reconsider the role they play in your life. Healthy relationships leave you feeling accepted and valued, not anxious or insecure.

If you recognize that a relationship is hurting you, the next step takes courage: setting boundaries or stepping away. That might mean having a difficult conversation. It might mean saying no more often. It might even mean asking for help. Whether it's from a parent, a teacher, a school counselor, or a trusted friend, reaching out can help you navigate these moments with more clarity and support. No one should have to face that kind of pain alone.

There may be times when the best decision is to walk away. That doesn't make you weak. It makes you wise. When you recognize consistent negativity, criticism, manipulation, or control, these are clear indicators that a relationship may be unhealthy. You might want to gradually reduce contact and communication with the person, setting boundaries that protect you. When you choose your well-being over someone else's approval, you're practicing self-love in action. Surround yourself with people who respect you, who listen without judgment, and who celebrate your growth. That's the kind of circle that helps you thrive.

I'd like to tell you about Natalie, a friend from my high school days. She was tall and thin, and a bit of a nerd like me. She used to light up every room she walked into, always smiling and saying funny things. But after a while, I noticed something had shifted. She wasn't eating when we were together. She'd brush it off or apologize if she took a bite. Her face looked more tired. Her smile didn't reach her eyes anymore. Slowly, she started pulling away from the group.

One day, I saw her at the mall with another girl who wasn't part of our circle. Natalie looked empty. I didn't say anything at the moment, but the next day, I asked if she was okay. She said she had tried on some clothes that didn't fit and was frustrated with herself for "being fat." But she wasn't fat at all. She was shrinking, physically and emotionally.

I invited her to come home with me after school to help me with a project. Once we were away from school, I gently asked her more questions. She opened up. This other friend had been feeding her comments for months, criticizing how she looked, suggesting she shouldn't eat certain things, and even questioning our friend group's loyalty. It had started with comments like, "Are you really going to eat *all* that?" and graduated to even more direct ones like, "You shouldn't eat that, you already look bigger than when I first met you". And Natalie had started believing her. The constant negativity had worked its way into her mind.

I helped her talk to our school counselor. Over the next few weeks, she opened up to her parents and got the support she needed. She gradually rebuilt her relationship with food, with us, and with herself. And she stopped seeing that girl altogether. It was eye-opening to realize how damaging toxic friendships can be and how easily they can go unnoticed from the outside.

That experience has stayed with me ever since. It reminded me of how fragile we can become as a consequence of someone else's judgment, and how much power lies in choosing the people who get to stay in your life. If anyone makes you feel bad about your body, your friends, your family, or your identity, pause and ask yourself: *Does this come from love or control?* Don't let harmful words settle into your sense of self. You deserve friendships that feed your spirit, not ones that silence it.

## Nurturing Friendships: Investing in Genuine Connections

Picture having a few close friends who truly get you, rather than a crowd of people who barely know your favorite song or what makes you laugh. Deep, meaningful friendships are rare, and that's what makes them so valuable. They provide a space where you can be fully yourself without pretense or inhibition. When you're with the right people, you don't have to perform. You just get to exist and feel accepted for it.

Genuine friendships offer more than companionship. They protect your mental health, give you a sense of belonging, and help you feel less alone in a world that sometimes moves too fast. When your friendships are rooted in trust, they become a safe space where you can share your thoughts, fears, and dreams without worrying about being judged.

However, just like any significant relationship, these relationships require care and attention. They don't grow strong by accident. You have to put in the time and effort. Just like a plant needs sunlight and water to thrive, friendships need time, consistency, and kindness. That could mean texting a friend just to say you're thinking of them, remembering their birthdays without a reminder, or showing up when it matters. Sometimes, it's as simple as making time to hang out, going for a walk, or staying in and laughing over nothing at all.

Sometimes, though, friendships shift. You grow. Your friends grow. And not every connection will grow in the same direction. That's okay. It's not about blaming anyone. It's about noticing when a friendship no longer supports your well-being. Maybe it used to, but now it feels one-sided, drained, or disconnected. Perhaps you've outgrown particular dynamics, or maybe your values no longer align. These realizations can feel uncomfortable, but they're essential. Letting go of friendships that don't serve you anymore can make room for the ones that do. You're not being unkind. You're being honest. And honesty is part of self-respect. Ask yourself: Does this friend celebrate my wins without competition? Do I feel lighter or heavier after spending time with them? Can I be my whole self, or do I feel like I have to hide parts of who I am? Your answers will guide you. Trust them.

I've experienced this more than once, and it's never easy. Sometimes, it feels like grief. I've had to step back from friendships that felt one-sided or emotionally draining. And even when I knew it was the right thing, I still felt like the worst person in the world for ending the friendship. I remember talking to my therapist at the time, trying to explain the guilt I felt. She looked at me and said, "Would you put your life on hold just to maintain a relationship that's not only draining you but also not helping her grow, either? You just told me you don't like who you are when you're with her, and you want to be better for yourself. Is staying in that friendship an act of love toward yourself?" That question stayed with me.

I still think of that person sometimes, and yes, I still feel that sting of guilt. Like I should've stuck it out, even at the cost of my peace, but when those thoughts creep in, I remind myself: it's okay to choose yourself. You are allowed to walk away from relationships that hurt more than they help. You are allowed to prioritize your well-being. Please keep that in mind.

You don't need a hundred friends. You need the ones who bring out the best in you. The ones that stay when it's hard. They cheer when you rise and help you remember who you are when you forget. When you invest in those kinds of friendships, you're not just building relationships; you're building your foundation.

## Communicating with Confidence: Expressing Yourself Clearly

Think about a time when you were sitting with a friend, sharing stories, laughter, and maybe even a few secrets. At the center of these moments is communication–the way you connect, listen, and express who you are. When you communicate well together, it deepens your relationships and helps you feel truly seen and understood. It starts with listening. Not just hearing the words but paying attention. Active listening means putting away distractions and focusing on the person in front of you. You nod, make eye contact, and show them you care about what they're saying. That kind of listening builds trust. It tells someone, "I'm here. I value what you have to say."

Your body language also matters. It communicates just as much as your words. When your posture is open, you look someone in the eye, or you give a small, supportive smile, you're telling them they're safe to open up. Your tone of voice adds another layer. A soft, calm tone can invite honesty. A sharp one can shut it down. Being aware of how you say something is just as important as what you're saying.

Sometimes, repeating what the other person said in your own words can be a helpful tool to show that you are listening. This skill is called paraphrasing, and it indicates that you're trying to understand. You might say, "So what you're feeling is..." or "It sounds like what you needed was..." These simple phrases can help avoid misunderstandings and make people feel heard.

When you learn to communicate clearly, your friendship grows stronger. You build mutual respect. You avoid minor issues from turning into big ones. When communication breaks down, even close friendships can feel fragile.

Take 15-year-old Zara and her best friend, Ariana. They'd been close for years, but one day, Zara noticed Ariana acting distant. Instead of asking what was going on, Zara assumed her friend was mad and started pulling back, as well. Their texts become shorter. They stopped hanging out like they used to. Weeks passed, and the distance grew. Eventually, Zara's mom asked her what was going on between them. Zara said she didn't know, and her mom asked, "Well, did you ask her?" Zara reached out, and Ariana told her she'd been feeling overwhelmed and hurt that Zara didn't check in. Zara realized she had jumped to conclusions instead of simply talking to her friend.

This kind of misunderstanding happens more often than you'd think. Sometimes, the fear of conflict or worry that you'll say the wrong thing makes it easier to avoid the conversation altogether. But that only builds more tension. If Zara had opened up earlier, if she had asked, "Hey, are you okay? You seem a little off lately," things might have been cleared up before the friendship got strained.

Learning to communicate with care doesn't mean you always get it right the first time. It means being willing to try, listen, and stay curious rather than making assumptions. Even when things go wrong, honest communication gives you a chance to reconnect and, sometimes, even grow closer because of it.

Disagreements are a natural part of every relationship. What matters is how you handle them. Before a tough conversation, take a moment to slow down and gather your thoughts. Think about how you're feeling and what you want to say. Clarity gives you confidence. You don't need to rehearse every word. Just focus on honesty and respect.

Even when emotions are high, your tone and posture can help keep things grounded. A calm voice. An open stance. Gentle eye contact. These things tell the other person, "I care. I want to work through this." A small gesture, like a nod or placing your hand over your heart, can communicate more than words ever could. It's okay to feel nervous. Being direct doesn't mean being harsh. You can express your feelings with kindness and still stand your ground.

Not every disagreement ends perfectly, and that's okay. But you can soften most conflicts with empathy and patience. When you approach challenging moments with honesty and care, you create space for understanding. And even if you don't agree with everything, your friendship can come out stronger because of it.

## Setting Boundaries with Grace: Protecting Your Peace

Understanding boundaries is like discovering the quiet superpower behind healthy relationships and deep self-respect. Boundaries are the invisible lines that protect your time, energy, and emotional well-being. They help you avoid overextending yourself or getting pulled into situations that don't feel right. Think of them as gentle, clear ways of saying, "This is where I end and someone else begins." They're not walls to shut people out. They're bridges that keep your connections strong and balanced.

Setting boundaries starts by noticing what makes you feel safe, respected, and true to yourself. It might be that you need alone time after a busy week, choose not to share certain parts of your life online, or step away from conversations that make you uncomfortable. Emotional boundaries might mean not taking on someone else's stress. Physical ones might include asking for space when you need it. And digital boundaries? They matter, too. In a world where your phone is always within reach, knowing when to unplug is an act of self-care.

Once you know your limits, the next step is speaking them aloud. That can feel intimidating at first. But it doesn't have to be harsh. It just has to be honest. If someone invites you to join something online that doesn't feel right with you, you might say, "Thanks for thinking of me, but that's not really my thing." Or if a friend wants to hang out every weekend but you need time to rest, you could say, "I love spending time with you, but I also need a day to recharge." Setting a boundary doesn't mean you care less about other people. It means you care about yourself, too.

14-year-old Maya found this out the hard way. Her best friend called or texted her constantly and got upset if Maya didn't respond right away. At first, Maya felt guilty and tried to keep up with her best friend. But over time, it started to wear her down. She began feeling anxious whenever her phone buzzed. Eventually, Maya talked to her friend and said, "I care about you a lot, but I also need time to focus on school and my own things. I won't always be able to respond right away, and I need you to be okay with that." Her friend didn't love hearing that, but Maya felt a weight lift. She had drawn a boundary that gave her room to breathe.

Sometimes, when you set a boundary, people won't like it. They might guilt-trip you, question your choices, or act distant for a while. That's not a sign you're doing something wrong. It's a sign you're doing something necessary. Staying calm and consistent is key. You can repeat your boundary kindly, like saying, "I know this is hard to hear, but this is what I need right now." The more often you stand by your limits, the more natural it becomes. And the more respect you gain from both others and yourself.

Boundaries take practice. You might wobble at first. You might second-guess yourself. That's okay. Every time you say no with clarity or step back when something doesn't feel right, you're building a habit of protecting your peace. And peace is something you deserve.

## Empathy and Understanding: Bridging Differences

Think about a time when you felt truly heard. A time when someone didn't just listen but understood what you were going through. That's empathy. It's not about fixing or advising. It's about showing up, feeling with someone, and letting each other know that all emotions are valid. Empathy builds trust. It deepens relationships. It reminds someone that they're not alone.

Maybe your friend tells you they've had the worst day ever. They failed a test, got into an argument with their parents, and just felt like giving up. It can be tempting to jump in with advice or try to lighten the mood. But empathy asks you to slow down. Instead of saying, "It's not that bad," or "You'll be fine," you might simply say, "That sounds really tough. I'm here for you." Those few words can make a huge difference.

Empathy isn't just a feeling. It's a skill. And like any skill, you can practice it. You can ask open-ended questions that create space for real answers. "What do you think would help?" or "What else could you tell me about it so that I can understand it better?" are better than yes-or-no questions. These kinds of conversations invite people to open up at their own pace, without pressure. Also, pay attention to non-verbal cues, the things someone might not say out loud. Their body language, tone of voice, or facial expressions can give you insight into how they're feeling. Responding to these cues with calmness and kindness shows you're paying attention.

Empathy is potent in moments of tension or conflict. When you're upset or hurt, it's easy to assume the worst about someone else's intentions. But taking a breath and asking, "What might they be doing through?" can shift your entire perspective. When you approach disagreements with a willingness to understand rather than just defend your point, it opens the space for connection and healing. Working together on a shared goal, such as a school project, a team sport, or a creative challenge, can also foster empathy. You learn how others think, what stresses them out, and how they shine. It helps you respect their strengths and see things from their side.

16-year-old Sofia had a falling out with her close friend Marisol. They'd snapped at each other during a group project and hadn't talked in days. Instead of staying angry, Sofia sat with it and realized Marisol had been under a lot of pressure at home. She reached out and said, "I think I took what you said the wrong way. I know you've had a lot going on. Can we talk?" That one message opened the door to an honest conversation. They both shared how they'd been feeling, and their friendships grew even stronger.

That's the power of empathy. It doesn't mean you'll always agree or avoid conflict. But it gives you a way to stay open, connected, and human with each other, even when things get messy. Practicing empathy doesn't just improve your relationships. It makes *you* feel more grounded, more compassionate, and more connected to the people around you.

## Building a Support Network: Friends, Family, and Community

Think of a support network as a safety net, something steady to catch you when life feels overwhelming. Your support network can include friends, family, teachers, coaches, mentors, and even online communities. These are the people who help you feel seen and encouraged. When you surround yourself with supportive people, you build emotional resilience. You feel more confident facing challenges because you know you're not going through them alone.

Support can take many forms. A best friend who listens without judgment. A sibling who makes you laugh after a tough day. A teacher who believes in your potential and pushes you to try. These people create a circle of care around you. They celebrate your wins, help you process your losses, and remind you of your worth.

Having a variety of connections makes your support system even stronger. Family and close friends can offer comfort and emotional stability. Mentors such as teachers or school counselors can provide advice, encouragement, and a broader perspective. Sometimes, just knowing you have someone to turn to makes all the difference.

Building meaningful connections takes time and intention. Try joining a club or group that matches your interest, whether that's art, robotics, music, dance, or a sport. Volunteering is another excellent way to meet people who share similar interests. Even attending a local event or support group can help you feel part of something bigger. These moments, even if they seem small at first, lay the foundation for genuine connection.

15-year-old Aisha felt isolated after moving to a new school. She missed her old friends and didn't feel like she fit in. But she decided to join the drama club, even though she'd never acted before. Over time, the rehearsals turned into friendships, and she found people who encouraged her, laughed with her, and checked in when she seemed off. That one decision gave her a new sense of belonging and reminded her that connection takes courage, but it's always worth the risk.

Pay attention to the people who lift you. To the ones who ask how you're doing and really listen. The ones who support your goals, respect your boundaries, and want the best for you. These are the people who deserve space in your life. At the same time, recognize when an adult might become a mentor, someone you trust to give advice and support, especially when things feel complicated.

When life gets heavy, reaching out isn't a weakness; it's wisdom. Sometimes, you need a friend to talk to. And sometimes, you might benefit from professional support like a therapist or counselor. These resources aren't just for crisis moments. There are tools available that help you care for your mental health and stay grounded when things get tough. Building a support network isn't about having tons of people in your life. It's about having the *right* people, those who show up, lift you, and help you grow.

***

## Hey, can I ask you something?

You're almost halfway through this book. If you're enjoying this book so far. If something in these pages has made you feel seen, understood, or hopeful, would you take a moment to share it? Make it your good deed of the day.

Books like this grows because of people like you. Through word of mouth. Through honest words. And your voice truly matters. When you share what this book meant to you, someone else might discover it at exactly the right time.

**Your words could be the reason another girl picks up this book and realize she's not alone.** Be the reason she starts her own self-love journey.

Even a few honest lines can make a real impact. It only takes a minute, and it means more than you know.

Thank you for being here.
Thank you for reading.
Thank you for being part of this.

**If you're open to helping, here's how:**

**Scan the QR code**

**Write what feels true to you**

**Thank you so much**

@THESELFLOVECOMPASS

SCAN ME

CHAPTER SIX

# Balancing Expectations and Personal Aspirations

"I tell my story not because it is unique,
but because it is the story of many girls."
Malala Yousafzai

Let's say you're at the dinner table, and someone brings up your future: college, career, and weekend plans. The conversation picks up speed, and suddenly, you feel caught in a whirlwind of opinions and expectations. You might be excited, but also a little tense or even rebellious.

Family dynamics shape how you see yourself and your dreams. Whether you're part of a nuclear family, living with a single parent, or surrounded by a big extended family, each setup contains its own rules, routines, and expectations. Understanding those dynamics helps you figure out how to stay true to yourself while still respecting the people who raised you and those who raised them.

Family beliefs and values often shape our perspective on success, responsibility, and even our identity. Maybe there's a long line of engineers in your family. Or perhaps you're expected to help out a lot at home because you're the oldest sibling. These patterns and expectations, whether spoken or unspoken, can influence the choices you make.

Cultural traditions can add even more layers of complexity. They can bring comfort and pride, but also pressure, especially if your personal goals feel different from what you feel is expected. Finding your path doesn't mean turning your back on where you came from. It's about honoring your roots while building a life that reflects who you are.

Navigating family relationships takes patience. Every family member has their own background and unique perspective on the world. It's normal for perspectives to differ, especially across generations. You might value mental health, while your parents grew up believing that they should keep emotions private. Or you might want to explore a creative career path that feels unfamiliar to them. The key is respectful communication. When you make space to listen and share, you create a bridge between your world and theirs.

Family conflict often happens when those bridges feel broken. You might feel like your parents don't understand what you're going through. Maybe they dismiss your stress or push expectations that feel too heavy. These moments can feel frustrating and lonely, but they're also an invitation to grow. Start by figuring out what the real issue is. Is it about grades? Curfews? Your future? Then, take a step toward an open dialogue. Expressing your needs clearly, calmly, and honestly gives your family a chance to hear you, and it also shows them that you're growing into your voice.

I get that this chapter might feel challenging. You're already juggling school, friends, emotions, and your inner changes, so adding family expectations into the mix might feel like too much. That's okay. You don't have to have it all figured out right now, or do it all at the same time. If something here doesn't feel right yet, bookmark it and come back to it when you're ready. The goal isn't to be perfect. It's to keep learning how to stay true to yourself, even when things feel complicated.

## Reflection Exercise: Bridging Generational Gaps

Think back to a recent family discussion that led to some tension. Maybe it was about school, responsibilities, or your future plans. Reflect on the different perspectives that they shared, especially the ones that clashed with your own. What did you hear? What didn't get said? Take a moment to write down how you felt in that moment and what you wish you had expressed. This is not about blaming anyone. It's about understanding where your feelings come from and how they connect to your values and needs.

Now, consider what steps you could take to bridge the gap. Could you start a calm conversation and ask questions about their perspective or find common ground on something you both care about? Sometimes, the smallest opening, like asking for their thoughts or explaining how something makes you feel, can begin to shift a conversation.

These family dynamics aren't just part of your past. They're part of your identity. They shape how you communicate, what you value, and how you connect with others. As you move forward, remember that it's not about choosing between your family and yourself. It's about finding a balance and honoring your roots while also embracing your individuality.

## Balancing Pleasing Others and Pursuing Passion

Let's say you're sitting down with your parents to discuss your future. It may feel daunting, but an open dialogue is the key to understanding one another. To prepare for family discussions, gather your thoughts and outline your aspirations. Clearly expressing your personal goals helps your parents appreciate your perspective and ambitions. Regular family meetings can create a consistent space for these conversations, allowing everyone to voice their thoughts without feeling rushed or judged. Even something as simple as family dinners can become platforms for meaningful discussions, where you share your dreams while listening to their concerns. This ongoing dialogue builds trust and ensures everyone feels heard.

Negotiation is not about getting your way or giving in, but about finding common ground where personal desires and parental expectations intersect. It's about compromise and mutual understanding. By setting achievable and shared family goals, you can align your plans with your family's values, creating a path that respects both perspectives.

Techniques for communicating your aspirations may include using "I" statements to express your feelings and needs, such as "I feel passionate about studying art because it allows me to express myself." This approach emphasizes your connection to your goals, helping your parents see things from your perspective.

Unrealistic expectations can negatively impact your mental health, leading to stress and affecting your self-esteem. When you feel pressured to meet specific standards, it can create a sense of inadequacy and anxiety. Understanding this dynamic is crucial for both you and your parent or parents. By addressing these expectations openly, you can work together to establish more realistic and supportive goals. Remember, the aim is to foster an environment where you feel empowered to pursue your dreams while maintaining a healthy and balanced relationship with your family.

## Pursuing Personal Dreams with Confidence

Take some time to think about what success looks like for you - not what you think it *should* look like, but what excites you. Maybe it's building a career around something you love, exploring the world, or becoming good at a skill that brings you joy. Whatever it is, it's yours to define. Success doesn't have to follow anyone else's blueprint. It's okay if your dream doesn't match what your family or friends expect. When you take time to reflect on what truly matters to you, you give yourself permission to build a life aligned with your values and passions.

Start by noticing what lights you up. What are you drawn to? What activities make you lose track of time? The things that spark your curiosity and energy can offer clues about your purpose. Exploring these interests can help you set goals that feel meaningful rather than just impressive on the surface. One way to bring those goals to life is by creating a vision board. Find images, quotes, and words that inspire you and represent the future you're working toward, and stick them on a piece of paper. Hang it somewhere visible so it can remind you why you're choosing your path, especially on hard days. You can also write a personal mission statement–a short, powerful sentence that captures what matters to you. It doesn't have to be perfect, and it can change as you grow. It's simply a reminder of what you stand for.

The truth is, the path to your dreams won't always be smooth. You'll face doubts–your own and other people's. Maybe someone questions your choices or makes you second-guess yourself. Perhaps you start comparing your progress to someone else's. These moments can feel discouraging, but they don't have to stop you. Reach out to someone who believes in you, such as a friend, teacher, family member, or mentor. A few kind words from the right person can make a big difference. Keep reminding yourself why your dream matters.

Think of someone like Aria, 16, who loved baking and dreamed of opening her own bakery. Some classmates teased her, saying it was a "silly hobby," but she kept practicing. She started a small business from home, selling cupcakes to friends and neighbors. Over time, her confidence grew. So did her customer list. What began as a passion turned into a real business. Aria's story is a reminder that believing in yourself and taking action, even in small steps, can turn a dream into something tangible.

Whatever your goals may be, know this: they don't need to be big to be meaningful. What matters is that they come from you. Be proud of your vision. Trust your voice. Keep showing up for yourself, even when it's hard. You're building something powerful.

## Time Management for a Balanced Life

Think of time as a canvas. Each day, you get to choose what you paint onto it. Managing your time isn't about cramming as much as possible into every hour; it's about creating space for what truly matters. That means organizing your day in a way that supports your priorities, energy, and peace of mind. One of the best places to start is by creating a simple daily schedule. Whether you use a planner, a digital calendar, or sticky notes, find a system that feels manageable and clear. Block out time for schoolwork, family, friends, hobbies, and rest, yes, rest counts, too.

One tool that can help you feel less overwhelmed is the Eisenhower Matrix. It's a way to sort your to-do list using four categories:

1. Do it now (urgent and important)
2. Schedule it (important but not urgent)
3. Delegate it (urgent but not important)
4. Let it go (not urgent and not important)

This helps you focus on what truly matters instead of stressing over everything at once. Think of it like packing for a weekend trip. You don't bring everything you own. You choose what's essential, what can wait, and what you don't need at all. When planning your week, ask yourself: *What needs to happen today? What supports my goals? What can be skipped or wait?*

Time management also means making room for the things that fuel you. When you have a clear plan, it becomes easier to balance responsibilities with the things that bring you joy. You're not just reacting to your day. You're directing it. Over time, this creates a sense of balance where school, fun, friendships, and the rest can coexist without chaos.

Tracking how you spend your time can be eye-opening. Some people like using apps, while others prefer writing things down. One helpful method is bullet journaling. It's a mix between a planner, a to-do list, and a diary. It's designed by you, for you. You use bullet points, symbols, and short notes to quickly track what you need to do, how you feel, or anything else that matters to you. There are no rules. You can keep it simple or decorate it with doodles, colors, or quotes. Some people use it to plan homework and self-care routines. Others track their sleep, mood, or habits. Over time, it helps you notice patterns about what's working, what's draining you, and where your time actually goes. Most of all, it's a flexible way to stay grounded, focused, and in charge of your day.

I use both my Google Calendar and a personalized journal. The calendar helps me keep track of my meetings and deadlines. My journal is where I break things down: detailed tasks, reflections, or little wins. I've realized there's no one perfect method. What works tends to shift as I grow, and that's okay. I once read that starting your day with two "wins" can help set the tone, and I started implementing this into my morning routine. The wins don't have to be something big. Some days, my morning meditation and a glass of water feel like wins. On other days, it's a short workout or showing up to my desk on time.

Try figuring out what small daily wins help you feel grounded. They don't need to be the same every day. You just need something that gives you a sense of accomplishment early on. I also only keep three main goals visible at a time. Once those are achieved, I set three more. Otherwise, I get lost in a never-ending to-do list, and that gets overwhelming fast.

Managing your time is really about honoring your energy and your goals. When you learn to do that, you build a daily rhythm that supports your growth and makes space for the things that matter most to you.

## Peer Pressure: Standing Strong in Your Values

The following might sound familiar: You're standing in a circle of friends, and everyone seems to agree on something you're not entirely comfortable with. Some are nudging you to join in, others are watching, and you feel that quiet tug–the need to go along so you don't stand out. Peer pressure comes in many forms. Sometimes, it's loud and obvious, like someone daring you to try something risky. At other times, it's more subtle, like feeling you have to dress a certain way, laugh at a joke you don't think is funny, or stay silent when you disagree. This pressure to conform can affect your choices, chip away at your confidence, and make it harder to trust your voice.

Recognizing peer pressure isn't always easy. Sometimes it hides in ordinary moments. A friend might make you feel guilty for saying no. Someone might say, "Don't be boring," or "It's not a big deal," even though it feels like a big deal to you. These kinds of comments can wear down your instincts. That's why self-awareness is crucial. Take a second to check in with yourself. Does this choice reflect your values, or are you doing it to avoid judgment? Ask yourself: If I were alone, would I still make this choice?

Standing up for yourself while keeping your friendships takes practice. At moments like this, assertiveness becomes a tool you can lean on. Assertive communication is clear, calm, and respectful–it's not about being rude or shutting others down. It's about standing in your truth. Try practicing what you'd say in challenging situations. For example: "I'm not into that, but I understand that you would really enjoy it," or "I'd rather sit this one out." These phrases are powerful. You can also role-play with a trusted friend or adult to build confidence in using your voice.

It helps to have support. Talk to someone you trust, a parent, sibling, teacher, or mentor, about what peer pressure feels like for you. One helpful tip is to create a "get-out" plan with an adult for situations where you feel really uncomfortable. It would help if it could be with a parent. This "get-out" plan could be a code word or a specific phrase in a text like "Can I pretty please," or "Just hear me out." You both agree that when you use that phrase or code word, it means you need help getting out of a situation. That adult can then call or text you with an excuse or come pick you up, giving you an easy way to leave without feeling like you have to explain yourself to anyone. It's the adults' "fault," not yours. It's not about being sneaky. It's about staying safe and having someone in the corner.

The truth is, staying true to yourself can feel hard in the moment, but every time you make a decision that honors your values, you become stronger. Peer pressure doesn't define you. You define yourself. And with practice, support, and courage, you'll keep growing into someone you're proud to be.

## Navigating School Dynamics: Thriving, Not Just Surviving

Chances are, you've seen this before: a busy school hallway where different cliques and social groups form a complex web of interactions. Each group has its own identity and vibe. Finding your place in all of that can feel both exciting and overwhelming. You might feel pressure to fit in or a pull to stand out, all while trying to figure out who you are. It can feel like trying to dance, where everyone moves to different beats. Understanding these dynamics is vital to a beat that constantly changes. But here's the truth: understanding these dynamics is helpful, and more importantly, you have the power to shape your experience. You're not here just to survive school. You're here to thrive.

Start by seeking connections outside your usual circle. Joining clubs, sports, or interest-based groups gives you the chance to meet people you might not talk to otherwise. When you get involved in activities that matter to you, you naturally attract others who share your values or interests. You might discover new friendships, new strengths, and even a new sense of belonging. And when you support inclusive efforts, such as clubs that celebrate culture, promote mental health awareness, or offer peer mentorship programs, you help create a school culture that makes *everyone* feel more welcome.

Of course, school isn't always smooth sailing. Conflict is a part of life, but learning how to resolve it peacefully is one of the best skills you can develop. Practicing empathy and active listening helps you see beyond your personal perspective and approach disagreements with curiosity rather than defensiveness. When you stay calm, express yourself clearly, and seek compromise, you build respect on both sides. It's not about avoiding all tension. It's about learning how to move through it with confidence and maturity.

Advocating for yourself is also part of thriving. That means speaking up when something doesn't feel right, whether you're dealing with unfair treatment, being left out, or experiencing bullying. Your voice matters. You deserve to feel safe and supported at school. Building positive relationships with teachers, school counselors, or mentors can help you navigate challenges. These adults can offer perspective, listen without judgment, and help you take steps toward solutions.

I want to share something personal with you. When I went to junior high school, I was bullied for being a nerd. I was basically like Hermione Granger with frizzy hair, minus the magical world, and yes, I wore glasses, too. My classmates thought it was hilarious to mock the smart girl in class because she wasn't "cool." They made fun of my clothes, my answers, and even the way I talked. It was petty and mean, and it made school a nightmare for me.

When it came time for senior high, I was terrified to be around those same kids again. I dreaded it so much that just thinking about it made me physically sick. My mom saw what I was going through, and she went to great lengths to get me into a different school. That change gave me a clean slate. I even got contact lenses to ditch the glasses that had haunted me for years. And it made a difference. I met people who saw me for who I was. Some of them remain my closest friends to this day.

I know not everyone has the option to switch schools, but what matters most is this: that experience doesn't define me. What they said, what they thought, it doesn't hold power anymore. *What do I believe about myself? That's what defines me.* You're not here to be anyone but yourself. That truth, and the way you carry it, is what will help you thrive.

So, if you're dealing with tough school dynamics right now, please remember this saying, "hurt people, hurt people." It means that people who have experienced being hurt, might end up hurting other people. You would need to make a conscious choice to let it stop there. Make sure that you don't follow the same cycle.

## Media Literacy: Critically Consuming Content

Today, we're surrounded by information–scrolling through feeds, watching videos, and reading headlines. That's why media literacy is more important than ever. It's about being an intelligent, thoughtful consumer of content. It means learning to look beyond the surface, asking questions, and understanding that not everything you see or hear is the whole truth. Media is often created with specific intentions, and those intentions shape how stories are told. Sensational headlines might be designed to get clicks rather than share facts. Influencers might promote products not because they love them but because they're paid to do so. Understanding this helps you take back control over what you believe and how you respond.

Start by getting curious. When you come across a piece of content, it can be an article, a post, or even a meme. Ask yourself: Who created this? What message are they trying to send? Is there a hidden agenda? Who benefits from me believing this? These questions help you spot media bias and manipulation. Sensationalism might make something seem more dramatic than it is. Gender portrayals and stereotypes often reinforce outdated ideas about how people "should" look, act, or think. And then there are images, so many of them digitally altered, that can distort your sense of what's normal or real.

Fact-checking is a powerful tool. If something seems shocking or hard to believe, don't just share it–research it. Use credible sources to double-check information. Examine the organization behind the message and its history of trustworthy reporting. You might also start to notice how algorithms affect what you see. Social media platforms track your clicks and interests to show you more of what you already like. While that can feel convenient, it can also create an echo chamber where you only see one point of view and miss out on broader perspectives.

That's why mindful media consumption matters. Think of it like your mental diet: if all you consume is fast, empty content, you won't feel great. Curate your feeds. Follow accounts that inspire you, educate you, and represent diverse voices. Unfollow those who leave you feeling inadequate or drained. Set boundaries, too. How much time are you spending scrolling? Are you checking your phone first thing in the morning or right before bed? If it feels like too much, it probably is.

Social media trends can move fast. One day, everyone's doing the same dance or challenge, and the next, there's a new viral opinion telling you what to think or feel. It's okay to enjoy trends, but always come back to your values. Ask yourself, "Does this really matter to me?" or "Do I agree with this, or am I just going along with it?" Taking a digital detox, whether for an hour, a day, or even a weekend, can help you reset. You step away, clear your mind, and return more grounded in your truth.

Being media literate doesn't mean you stop enjoying content. It means you engage with it on your terms. You're in charge of where you put your attention. You get to decide what influences you, what deserves your time, and what doesn't.

## Cultivating Self-Validation

Imagine standing in front of a mirror, looking at your reflection, and feeling a quiet sense of pride, not because someone else praised you, but because *you* know your worth. That's the core of self-validation: the practice of recognizing your value without waiting for others to confirm it. It means affirming your emotions and accomplishments, whether or not anyone else notices. When you stop relying on likes, comments, or approval from others to feel good about yourself, you begin to build a stronger, more grounded sense of identity.

Start by celebrating your wins, even the small ones. Maybe you helped a classmate, finished a complex project, or simply got through a tough day. These moments matter. Keep a journal where you write them down, not just the significant achievements, but also the quiet victories. Over time, this habit helps you track your growth and recognize the strength you already carry with you.

Gratitude can also strengthen your ability to validate yourself. Each day, list a few things you're thankful for. It can be things you did, choices you made, or moments that made you feel good. Connecting with gratitude shifts your focus from what's missing to what's meaningful. It reminds you that your life is already filled with value, even on ordinary days.

Equally important is self-compassion. That means talking to yourself with the same kindness you'd give a close friend. When you make mistakes, resist the urge to tear yourself down. Instead, acknowledge that everyone slips up. Mistakes don't define you. They help you grow. Being kind to yourself doesn't mean avoiding responsibility. It means choosing growth over shame.

Handling criticism can be tough, especially when it comes from people you care about or from your inner voice. Learn to tell the difference between feedback that helps you improve and comments that simply hurt. Constructive feedback can give you direction. Harsh criticism is maybe more difficult to navigate. When faced with either, return to your core. Repeat a personal mantra, such as *"I am capable and resilient."* Remind yourself of who you are and who you're becoming.

The more you validate yourself, the less power external judgment holds over you. You start showing up differently, with quiet confidence and unshakable self-worth. And that kind of inner strength? It's one of the most powerful things you can cultivate.

## Assertiveness: Respectfully Expressing Your Needs

Expressing your needs can sometimes feel like walking a tightrope–balancing honesty with kindness without slipping into conflict. That's where assertiveness comes in. It's not about being loud or demanding. It's about speaking your truth with clarity and respect, ensuring your voice is heard without compromising the voices of others in the process.

Think of assertiveness as the skill that lets you say what you need and stand up for yourself *without* being aggressive or passive. Have you ever worked on a group project, and your ideas kept getting brushed aside? Instead of staying silent or lashing out in this situation, you might say, "I feel like my ideas haven't been heard, and I'd really like to share." That one sentence does a lot. It puts your feelings out there without placing blame. It invites conversation rather than conflict. Pairing your words with confident body language, like steady eye contact and a calm tone, makes your message even stronger. You're not just speaking up. You're standing tall in your truth.

Still, the idea of being assertive can feel scary, especially if you're used to keeping the peace or avoiding conflict. The fear of rejection, judgment, or disappointing others is a genuine concern. That's why it helps to practice. Try role-playing situations where you need to be assertive, maybe with a trusted friend or in front of a mirror. Say the words out loud. Notice how your body feels. Each time you rehearse, you build the muscle of self-respect. It becomes easier to stand up for yourself when it matters.

Take the story of 15-year-old Mei, who kept getting invited to parties she didn't feel comfortable attending. At first, she made excuses. But eventually, she chose to be honest. She said, "Thanks for the invite, but that's not really my scene. I'd rather hang out in a smaller group." The reaction? Some people didn't get it, but others respected her for being clear. And most importantly, *she* felt proud of herself for listening to her gut. That moment became a turning point in how she valued her voice.

Assertiveness is not about winning or convincing everyone to agree with you; it's about showing up for yourself, even when it's uncomfortable. Every time you speak your truth with kindness and confidence, you reinforce a powerful message: *my needs matter, too.*

Chapter Seven

# Building Emotional Resilience and Well-Being

"If you are broken, you do not have to stay broken."
Selena Gomez

Have you ever watched a tree sway in the wind, bending but not breaking? That's resilience: your ability to adapt, bounce back, and stay grounded while going through challenges. It doesn't mean you never struggle. It means you find a way through. Like that tree, your roots–your values, support system, and inner strength–keep you steady, even in storms.

Think about a time when something didn't go as planned. Maybe you failed a test or felt left out. It hurt in the moment, but you eventually found your way forward. That's resilience in action. It's not about being tough all the time but about staying open to growth and finding strength in the struggle. People who build this skill don't avoid failure; they face it, learn from it, and come back stronger. And resilience isn't just emotional. It can also lower stress levels, improve focus, and support your physical health.

When you grow your resilience, you give yourself the tools to thrive, not just survive.

A resilient mindset starts with realistic goals and expectations. It's about knowing what you want to achieve and understanding that setbacks are part of the process. When you set achievable goals, you're not just reaching for the stars but also laying the groundwork for success. Consider 13-year-old Catalina, who struggled with math. Instead of aiming for perfection, she set a goal to improve her grade over a specific time. Each small victory built her confidence, teaching her that progress is more important than perfection. Cultivating a growth mindset is another key aspect. Having this mindset means believing that your abilities can develop through effort and learning. When you approach challenges with curiosity rather than fear, you open yourself to new possibilities. It's like viewing each obstacle as a stepping stone, not a roadblock.

Mindfulness can also strengthen resilience. It's not about clearing your mind or sitting cross-legged in silence. It's about being present. Whether you're taking a few deep breaths before a test or simply paying attention to what's happening around you, mindfulness helps you stay grounded. It gives you space to respond rather than react.

Reframing negative thoughts is another powerful strategy. When you catch yourself thinking, *"I'm going to mess this up,"* pause and ask, *"Is this fact or fear?"* Then, try to view the situation from a different angle. It's like looking at a rainy day and choosing to see how it nourishes the earth instead of focusing on the puddles. That shift in perspective changes everything.

## Reflection Exercise: Building Your Support Network

Take a moment to think about the people in your life who make you feel seen, safe, and supported. These are the ones who cheer you on, even when you doubt yourself. Write down their names. It can be friends, family members, mentors, or anyone who lifts you when you're down. This group of people is your personal support network. These are the people who remind you who you are when your confidence wavers.

Once you've made your list, reach out. Share your goals with the people who are important to you. Tell them how much their support means to you. Relationships deepen when you express appreciation, and it reminds people that they matter in your life, too. If you're still building your network, that's okay. Consider starting by joining an online group that aligns with your values and interests. A support system can begin with one honest conversation. Resilience isn't built on your own; it's nurtured in connection with people who see your worth even on the days you forget it.

I want to tell you about a Friday that hit me harder than I expected. I hadn't slept well and woke up feeling off. Then, a co-worker sent me feedback on a project I'd delivered. It was fair and constructive, but my tired brain twisted it into something harsher. What I *read* wasn't, "Here's how to improve." What I heard in my head was, "You are terrible at this. You shouldn't even be in this job." I cried through half the day, trying to work while my inner critic tore me down. When my partner came home and saw my face, he asked if I wanted to talk. I told him I felt like a complete fraud. Like I'd failed at something I cared about.

He hugged me and said, "You got feedback, you made improvements, and she said the next thing you delivered was better, right?" I nodded. "Okay," he continued, "so what's your next step?" I said, through tears, "Honestly? I want to wallow. This hurts." He nodded and replied, "Okay. Wallow today. But on Monday? You show them. Show *yourself*. You've got this." That moment stuck with me. Because I didn't need a pep talk, I needed someone to hold space for me and then remind me of my strength. That's what a sound support system does.

We all get knocked down at times. But getting up again is a choice. Improving is a choice. Cheering yourself on, especially when it's hard, is a choice. And having the right people around you makes all the difference. When your inner critic is too loud, your support system helps you hear your inner cheerleader again. It takes time to find those people. But when you do, hold them close. And be that person for others, too.

## Understanding and Managing Triggers: Tools for Calm

Have you ever found yourself sitting in class when the teacher suddenly announced a pop quiz? Your heart races, your hands go clammy, and a wave of panic starts to build. That rush of emotion? It's a trigger. It's your body's response to a stressor, often before your brain has even had time to process it. Emotional triggers are powerful. They can stem from anything–academic stress, a specific smell, a tone of voice, or a memory that bubbles up without warning. And they don't just affect your mood. They affect your body, too. It might be sweaty palms, a tight chest, or a sinking feeling in your stomach. The more you understand your triggers, the more control you gain over how you respond.

Start by becoming a detective in your own life. Pay attention to what sparks those intense emotional reactions. Keep a simple trigger journal for a week or two. When something hits hard, whether it's anxiety, anger, or shame, jot down what happened, how you felt, and what you noticed in your body. Over time, you'll see patterns. Maybe group projects make your stomach turn, or maybe crowded hallways make your chest tighten. These aren't just "random" bad moments. They're clues. Knowing your patterns gives you the power to plan, shift your mindset, and handle challenging moments with more ease.

Once you've spotted your triggers, the next step is to manage them. One simple technique is called four-square breathing. Breathe in for four counts, hold it for four, exhale for four, and then pause for four. Repeat a few times. It helps calm your nervous system and gives your brain a chance to catch up. It's not just about being calm, but coming back to yourself and feeling grounded. Grounded means steady, present, and connected to your body instead of spinning in fear or overthinking. It's that deep breath moment where you remember, *"I'm okay. I can handle this."* It may feel a bit odd, but it pulls you back into the present moment, where anxiety loses its grip on you.

I know, I know. Someone once told me, "Just breathe, and everything will be fine," and I wanted to roll my eyes so hard they got stuck. But now I understand the science. These tools I just mentioned really work, not because they're magic, but because they calm the physical panic, allowing your brain to think clearly again. Give them an honest try. If they don't work, that's okay. You'll find something that does.

Let me tell you about 15-year-old Indira, who used to panic before every school dance. The noise, the pressure to be social, the fear of being judged, it was overwhelming. But instead of avoiding them altogether, Indira started using visualization exercises beforehand. She'd take five minutes before leaving the house to breathe deeply, visualize the space, connect with how she wanted to show up for herself in that situation, and remind herself she could leave at any time if it got too much. Eventually, Indira was able to enjoy herself and even make new friends. Her triggers didn't disappear, but she stopped letting them control her.

Managing emotional triggers isn't about becoming "perfectly calm." It's about noticing your reactions and making choices that support your well-being–learning to control your triggers takes time, patience, and self-compassion. But with the right tools and people around you who support your growth, you'll find your way through.

## Positive Affirmations: Rewriting Your Inner Dialogue

Have you ever tried waking up, looking in the mirror, and saying something kind to yourself before your brain has the chance to criticize? That's the power of positive affirmations. They're short, powerful phrases that help you rewrite the script in your mind. Instead of repeating, "I'm not good enough," you start saying, "I am learning and growing." Over time, these words reshape how you see yourself. And yes, there's real science behind it. Your brain is constantly changing; this is known as neuroplasticity. When you practice affirmations regularly, you're literally training your brain to think in a more supportive, empowering way. It's not magic, but it can feel like it when that inner critic finally starts to quiet down.

To make affirmations truly work for you, you have to personalize them. Start by noticing the thoughts that put you down. Maybe it's "I always mess things up" or "Nobody likes me." These are the types of thoughts you'll rewrite. Use "I am" statements that feel true to the direction you're headed in. So, if you're working on growing your confidence, try: "I am growing more confident every day" or "I am proud of the effort I'm making." Keep your affirmations present-tense, positive, and meaningful. You might find it helpful to write a list of qualities you admire about yourself, or even ones you want to grow into, and build affirmations around them.

Need a little help getting started? Try these:

- I am worthy of love and respect.
- I am enough, exactly as I am.
- I am learning from my mistakes and getting stronger.
- I am proud of how far I've come.
- I am allowed to take up space and use my voice.

You can say them out loud in the mirror, write them in a journal, or even create a wallpaper for your phone. The more you repeat them, the more your brain starts to believe them. And if you want more ideas, make sure to grab the free mini-workbook by scanning the QR code in the beginning of the book, or buy the more comprehensive workbook.

Let me tell you about 16-year-old Zoe. She used to avoid speaking up in class because she was terrified of sounding "dumb." Every time she stayed quiet, her inner voice would say, "See? You don't belong here." But after a counselor suggested using affirmations, she started speaking to herself every morning, "I am smart. I deserve to be heard." At first, it felt awkward. But slowly, she noticed something shift. She raised her hand more. She felt more grounded. One day, her teacher even complimented her on her thoughtful question. Zoe didn't become fearless overnight, but those simple words helped her believe in herself when it mattered most.

Affirmations are not about pretending everything's perfect. They're about giving yourself the compassion and courage to grow. One kind phrase at a time: you can rewrite the way you speak to yourself–and change the way you show up in the world.

## Stress Management: Finding Your Peace

Life as a teen can feel like juggling a dozen balls while balancing on a moving skateboard. Schoolwork, sports, social plans, family expectations–it piles up fast. You're expected to keep your grades up, plan your future, show up for your friends, and somehow also have time for yourself. No wonder it feels like you're constantly behind or barely holding it together. Stress sneaks in and becomes the background noise in everything you do.

It helps to think of stress as your body's alarm system. It's trying to tell you something: slow down. Burnout isn't just being tired; it's the feeling that no matter how much you rest, you never fully recharge. You might snap at people more easily, lose interest in things you usually enjoy, or just feel numb. That's your cue. It's time to prioritize yourself. Rest and self-care aren't optional. They're how you recover, rebuild, get back in balance, and keep going. And when it gets to be too much, talking to someone–whether it's a friend, teacher, or therapist–is one of the strongest things you can do. You don't have to carry everything alone.

Managing stress starts with building a toolkit that works for you. Try progressive muscle relaxation. Tense one muscle group at a time, then slowly release the muscles. It helps you tune into your body and release the tension you might not even realize you're holding. Mindfulness meditation can bring calm in the chaos. Just a few minutes of deep breathing while focusing on the present moment can help reset your nervous system. Visualization is another option–picture a peaceful scene, like a forest or the ocean, and let your mind rest there for a bit.

Time management also plays a significant role. A lot of stress comes from feeling like there's never enough time. Use a planner or app to map out your day. Set specific study hours and breaks, and include time for things you enjoy. Don't overbook yourself just to please others; your well-being matters more than anyone else's expectations. And sleep? Sleep isn't just helpful. It's necessary. Prioritize it like you would an important appointment. Without rest, none of your stress tools will work as well as you'd like them to

Let me tell you about Bella, a 14-year-old straight-A student who also practiced dance five nights a week. On the outside, she looked like she had it all together. Inside, she was exhausted. She started skipping meals, snapping at her siblings, and crying at night without knowing why. After she fainted at school one day, she finally told her mom she couldn't handle everything anymore. They worked together to reduce her dance schedule, and Bella began journaling and practicing guided meditations before bed. It didn't fix everything overnight, but now she feels like she can breathe again. Her grades are still good, but more importantly, so is her mental health.

You don't have to earn rest. You're allowed to slow down. Make a list of the things that help you unwind–your stress relief playlist, a walk outside, sketching, dancing, or simply breathing deeply for one whole minute. Start building a plan that's yours. Protect your peace. It's not selfish. It's survival.

## Turning Setbacks into Comebacks: Resilience in Action

Here's a moment you might recognize: you study for weeks, give it your all, and still fail the test. Or you train hard for the team tryouts, only to see someone else take the spot. It feels like everything you worked for fell apart. But what if those moments weren't the end but the beginning of something better?

Setbacks aren't just failures. They are feedback. A setback is the starting point of a comeback. Think of Thomas Edison. He didn't get it right the first time or the hundredth. He failed over a thousand times before finally inventing the lightbulb. His mindset? Every failure was one step closer to success. That mindset is something you can build, too.

Take Serena Williams, one of the most accomplished athletes in the world. Her journey hasn't been easy. She's faced injuries, intense public scrutiny, and even life-threatening health issues after becoming a mom. But instead of letting those challenges define her, she used them to fuel her drive. She kept showing up, kept pushing forward, and proved that setbacks don't have to stop you. Her story is a reminder that resilience means rising, even when it's hard, and doing it on your terms.

Building resilience means setting goals that are within reach and then stacking small wins. That's what helped 13-year-old Camile, who was terrified of public speaking. Instead of aiming for a flawless speech, she started small. She practiced reading aloud to her sister. Then she gave a short talk in class. Eventually, she volunteered to speak at the assembly. It didn't happen overnight, but every small success helped her on the way and turned her fear into confidence.

Support systems matter here as well. Find your people. Maybe it's a teacher who believes in you, a friend who listens without judgment, or a parent who cheers you on. Lean on them. Let them remind you what you're capable of when you forget. And most of all, challenge the voice in your head that says you "can't." Replace it with: "I'm learning how to." That's at the core of a growth mindset, which doesn't pretend that setbacks don't hurt, but just refuses to let them stop you.

You might know someone like 15-year-old Tiana, who got bullied in middle school. For a while, it broke her confidence. But instead of letting it define her, she got involved in a youth advocacy group. She began speaking up for others, sharing her own story, and creating a safe space for classmates who felt isolated. What once made her feel small became her fuel to make a difference.

Your setbacks don't define the end of your story. They're the chapter that builds your strength, your voice, and your power. So the next time life knocks you down, remember, you get to write the comeback.

## The Art of Letting Go: Moving Past Negativity

Imagine carrying a backpack everywhere you go. But instead of books, it's full of invisible rocks–each one representing a grudge, a harsh comment, a moment that hurt you deeply. It's heavy and exhausting, and no one else can see it. That's what holding on to negativity feels like. The weight builds quietly until it emotionally drains you without even knowing why you feel so tired. Resentment, self-blame, and unresolved conflict don't just stay in your mind–they show up in your body, your mood, and your relationships. Letting go isn't about pretending things didn't happen. It's about choosing not to carry them anymore.

Letting go begins with recognizing what's holding you back. Visualization can be of great help here. Picture a balloon in your hand, one for every thought or emotion weighing you down. Maybe it's something someone said, a mistake you can't stop replaying, or a situation that left you feeling small. Then, one by one, imagine letting the balloons go. Watch them rise and float away. You're not forgetting. You're freeing up space for something lighter. You can also try a "letter release." Write down everything you need to say, pour your heart into it, and when you're done, tear it up or safely burn it. The act alone can be incredibly freeing.

Letting go also means forgiveness, but not in the way most people think. Forgiveness isn't about excusing someone's actions or pretending you're fine. It's about giving yourself peace. Start by forgiving yourself. Everyone makes mistakes, and none of them define you. You're allowed to grow, change, and try again. If someone else hurt you, writing a letter you don't send or simply meditating on a feeling of compassion (even just a flicker) can begin to loosen the emotional grip they have on you. Forgiveness is not approval. It's release. And it's for you, not them.

To support this process, try building simple rituals that help you reset and recharge. Light a candle when you're ready to move on. Or take a walk and imagine leaving pieces of the past behind with each step. Maybe create a playlist of songs that help you release and rise. Affirmations can also be powerful here. Repeat phrases like:"I am not my past." "I choose peace over pain." "I'm growing through what I've gone through."

Even if you don't believe them at first, keep going. Your brain listens. Over time, these affirmations become a new inner dialogue–stronger, kinder, and aligned with who you're becoming.

And yes, while writing this, I had "Let It Go" from *Frozen* stuck in my head. Honestly, when it came out in 2013, I didn't feel the lyrics the way I do now. But if you've never really *listened* to that song, or haven't heard it in a while, give it another shot. One line might hit differently now. It reminds me of moments I stayed quiet when I should've spoken up or when I finally decided to stop chasing validation. But mostly, it reminds me I can choose to let go, to stop dragging the weight of other people's opinions, mistakes, or limitations.

You're not meant to carry every heavy thing forever. Letting go is not a weakness. It's strength. It's healing. It's freedom. And you are more than ready. That backpack... it doesn't need to be full of pebbles, rocks, or anything heavy. You might not think so, yet, but you have the ability to let go of things that are not good for you, and it is okay to get some help in achieving this.

## Embracing Change and Uncertainty

Change is a constant part of life. Just like the seasons shift from winter to spring to summer to fall, your life moves through phases–some smooth, others more difficult. And yet, changes bring possibility. It opens doors to new people, new ideas, and new parts of yourself. It's okay to feel unsure when something changes. That nervous, fluttery feeling in your stomach? Totally normal. Whether you're starting a new school, moving to a different neighborhood, or trying something for the first time, it's all part of growing. Change might shake your routine, but it also gives you the chance to discover your strength.

One of the most effective ways to manage change is by setting flexible goals. Think of it like heading out on a trip. You might have a destination in mind, but you're open to taking scenic routes along the way. You're still moving forward, but you allow space to pivot. Practicing acceptance helps, too. It's not about liking everything that happens; it's about choosing not to fight the things you can't control. That decision to breathe and adapt makes a difference. When you shift your mindset from "Why is this happening?" to "What can I learn here?" you give yourself power. That one question can flip the entire experience. Suddenly, uncertainty becomes something to explore, not fear.

A positive mindset doesn't mean pretending everything is perfect. It means believing that even in tough times, growth is possible. Take 14-year-old Emma. She moved across the country just before her first year of high school. She didn't know anyone and spent the first week eating lunch alone. Instead of shutting down, she pushed herself to try something new and joined a school art club. Within a month, she'd made friends, entered a student exhibit, and discovered she loved digital painting. Emma didn't just "get through" the move, she grew because of it. Her story serves as a reminder that change can lead you somewhere better than you ever imagined.

## Gratitude Practices: Focusing on Positives Amidst Chaos and Finding Joy in Your Qualities

Life moves fast. School, social pressure, emotions–it's easy to get caught up in everything that's going wrong or what's missing. But what if you pressed pause for just a moment and noticed what's *right?* That's the power of gratitude. It's like a flashlight for your brain, helping you spot the good, even in the middle of chaos. Studies show that practicing gratitude can boost your mood, reduce anxiety, and help you feel more grounded. When you focus on the good, your brain releases feel-good chemicals, like dopamine and serotonin. That's science, those feel-good chemicals are real, powerful, and accessible to you every single day.

You don't need anything fancy to start. A simple notebook can become your gratitude journal. Each evening, write down three things you're thankful for–no matter how small. A good hair day. A friend who made you laugh. The sun finally showed up after days of rain. When you're writing these things down, feel that gratitude in your heart, and let that feeling stay with you as long as you're able.

Or try writing a letter to someone who's helped you, even if you don't send it. Gratitude jars are fun, too: each time something good happens, write it down and drop the piece of paper in the jar. Over time, you'll fill a jar full of reasons to smile. These small habits can gradually change the way you experience your day, your week, and, ultimately, your life.

Gratitude doesn't just help you appreciate others, it enables you to enjoy yourself. When you learn to focus on what you already have and who you already are, you stop chasing approval from the outside. It becomes less about needing others to tell you you're good enough and more about recognizing your worth from within. The next time you're being hard on yourself, flip the script. Instead of "I didn't do enough," say, "I showed up today, and that matters." That shift can change how you see yourself, not just as someone trying to measure up, but as someone already worthy.

13-year-old Chloe used to scroll through social media, feeling like she wasn't pretty or smart enough. But after starting a daily gratitude list in her notes app, something changed. At first, it felt weird, writing things like, "My cat curled up with me this morning" or "I liked my outfit today." But weeks later, she realized she was smiling more, and those negative thoughts weren't as loud anymore. She began to see the good, not just in her life, but in herself.

Gratitude won't make problems disappear, but it will help you face them with more peace, more confidence, and a stronger sense of who you are. And that's something to be grateful for.

## Chapter Eight

# Creative Expression as a Self-Love Practice

"You have to be unique and different
and shine in your own way."
Lady Gaga

### Art as Therapy

Picture a blank canvas in front of you. No rules. No pressure. Just space to feel. That canvas is yours to fill with color, with energy, with emotion. You don't need to be "artistic" or "talented" to use creativity as a way to heal. You just need to show up. This chapter examines how art can serve as a means of self-expression, emotional release, and enhanced self-understanding. Art therapy isn't about making something perfect. It's about letting yourself *feel* through your hands when words can't do the job. Whether you're painting, drawing, collaging, or sculpting, creative expression gives your emotions a way to be expressed.

Colors and shapes speak a language of their own. A bright yellow might lift your energy. A deep red might carry your frustration. A soft gray might gently hold your sadness. Even the shapes you create, sharp angles or soft curves, can reflect your inner world. When you slow down and pay attention to these choices, you start to understand what's going on beneath the surface. And you don't need to analyze every piece like a therapist would. You just need to notice. Using color and form as tools can help you express emotions that feel too complex to put into words.

Different art techniques offer various kinds of emotional release. Painting can help you calm your mind and body. The moment your brush hits the paper, you're present. There's no test. No pressure. Just movement and color. If you're feeling overwhelmed, painting gives you a place to channel that energy. If you're feeling stuck, collaging might help. Gathering words, pictures, and textures that speak to you can help you tell your story without having to explain everything. Every cut-out, every layered image is a snapshot of what matters to you.

Then there's sculpting. Working with clay or similar materials gives your hands something to do when your mind feels crowded. The act of molding something–shaping it, pressing into it, reworking it–can be incredibly grounding. You don't just see the art. You feel it. And through that process, you often uncover emotions you didn't know you were carrying. It's a slow, steady way to come back to yourself.

You don't need to make something "good." You just need to create something that's *true to you*. Creative expression is personal. It's powerful. And it's a practice of self-love.

## Activity: Personal Art Journal

Start your art journal, a space that's just for *you.* No grades. No rules. There's no pressure to make it look a certain way, just a place where your thoughts and emotions can land on the page in whatever form they take.

Grab a blank notebook, some colored pencils, markers, magazine clippings, or paint, whatever feels fun to work with. You don't need fancy supplies. What matters is that you feel free to experiment. One page might be covered in bold brushstrokes. Another might be a quiet sketch in pencil. You could try layering textures, mixing colors, writing words, or gluing down images that speak to you. Each page becomes a small snapshot of where your heart and mind are that day.

This journal is your safe zone. Let it hold your emotions without judgment. Use it when you feel overwhelmed, excited, frustrated, or just reflective. Maybe you draw a messy storm to get out your anger. Perhaps you use calming blues and soft lines to soothe anxiety. Whatever you create, trust that it matters, even if it doesn't make sense right away.

Over time, take a look back. What do you notice? Are there colors you return to often? Shapes or symbols that pop up again and again? This reflection helps you gain a deeper understanding of your emotional patterns. It's not about decoding everything, it's about connecting more deeply with yourself.

And if you ever feel ready, you can share your journal with someone you trust. Not for approval, but to open up a conversation. Sometimes, art says what words can't express. And sometimes, showing someone your pages can help you feel seen in a whole new way. This journal isn't just about art. It's about you showing up for *yourself*, one page at a time.

## Music and Movement: Dancing to Your Own Beat

Have you ever found yourself noticing that the world fades out as your favorite song fills your ears? The beat takes over, your foot starts tapping, and before you know it, your whole body's moving. That's the magic of music and movement. They have this incredible ability to shift your emotions, helping you process what you're feeling, without saying a single word.

Music can lift your mood, calm your nerves, or help you cry when you need a release. Science backs this up: music activates areas in your brain connected to emotion, memory, and mood. In short, it's like therapy wrapped in sound. You can start small. Create playlists that match different moods. One for joy, one for when you're anxious, one for when you want to feel powerful. Or explore new genres: lo-fi for focus, R&B for comfort, pop for energy. Let music become part of your emotional toolkit.

Then there's movement. Dance isn't just performance, it's expression. It's your body telling a story that your voice might not be ready to share. Dancing helps you process intense feelings, build confidence, and feel more at home in your body. You don't need a stage or choreography. Just close your door, turn up the music, and move. Freestyle, silly, serious–however it comes out is exactly how it needs to.

Want structure? Try a class or YouTube tutorial. Explore different styles: hip-hop, contemporary, ballet, or even cultural dances from your background. Not only do you get to learn something new, but you also connect with others who are also using movement as self-expression.

And remember this: there's a reason the phrase *"Dance like no one is watching"* sticks. There's freedom in it. I have a daily alarm on my phone, a song that instantly makes me feel energized. When it plays, I stop what I'm doing, get up, and dance. It takes four minutes, but it resets my whole mindset. It reminds me to choose my energy.

Try it for yourself. Pick a song that makes you feel alive, set a reminder, and let your body do what it wants. No rules. Just rhythm, release, and joy.

## Writing Your Truth: The Power of Words

Have you ever felt like your brain is spinning with thoughts that won't slow down? Like emotions are piling up, and you don't know where to put them? That's where journaling comes in. It's not about having the perfect words. It's about having a space that's just yours, where you can say anything without judgment. Journaling is like talking to the one person who always gets you: you.

Some days, you might write a few words. On other days, it's a whole page. It could be messy, emotional, hopeful, or just quiet. That's the beauty of it. And when you pair it with creativity, adding color, doodles, or symbols, you unlock a deeper layer. You give yourself permission to feel, express, and process in a way that words alone sometimes can't.

Start simple. Answer questions like:

- What made me smile today?
- What challenged me?
- What's the one thing I need to hear right now?

Or try stream-of-consciousness writing, where you write whatever comes to mind without editing or filtering. Let it all out. Don't worry about grammar, spelling, or making sense. Just write. Sometimes, clarity emerges from the chaos.

This practice helps you spot patterns in your emotions and reactions. The more you reflect, the more you understand what triggers you, what heals you, and what truly matters to you. And that awareness? It's powerful. It's how you grow more solid and softer at the same time.

Make journaling your ritual. Maybe it's part of your morning routine or something you do before going to bed. Light a candle. Put on soft music. Choose a notebook that feels special. Create a little space that feels like yours. Even five minutes a day can make a difference.

And don't be afraid to explore different styles:

- Stream of consciousness when you need a mental release.
- Gratitude journaling to shift focus from stress to joy.
- Prompts to go deeper when you feel stuck.
- Poetry when emotions are big, and words feel too sharp.
- Short stories to explore "what ifs" or express feelings through fiction.

Your journal isn't about being "good" at writing. It's about being real. It's a private space to become aware of your thoughts, hold space for your feelings, and track your growth. It's a mirror, and over time, you'll be amazed at what you see reflected.

## Creating a Vision Board: Mapping Your Future

What if you wake up and see your dreams laid out in front of you–goals, places, people, moments you haven't experienced yet but fully believe are possible? That's what a vision board does. It's more than just cutting out cute magazine pictures and sticking them on paper. It's your goals made visible. It's your future in progress.

A vision board helps you *see* your goals every day. Visualization is a powerful thing. Research indicates that mentally visualizing your success can enhance motivation and performance. So when you surround yourself by images and words that align with what you want most, you're not just hoping–you're programming your brain to move toward those goals with focus and intention.

Start by asking yourself: *What do I want more of in my life?* Maybe it's confidence, strong friendships, better grades, or travel. Then, grab your supplies–magazines, scissors, glue, and a poster board–or opt for digital tools like Canva or a vision board app. Pick out images, words, or quotes that match your goals. Don't overthink it. If something sparks a positive feeling, it belongs.

As you piece it together, you're doing more than decorating–you're declaring what matters to you. You're creating a visual compass that reminds you of the direction you're heading, even when the path gets bumpy. Your board might include:

- A photo of a school you dream of attending
- A quote that makes you feel brave
- A picture of a person confidently standing tall
- Words like "focus," "belonging," or "freedom"

Once your board is done, place it where you'll see it daily–on your wall, inside a notebook, next to your mirror, or even as your phone's lock screen. Let it remind you of what you're building and who you're becoming. And remember: your vision board isn't fixed. You're allowed to grow, change direction, or set new goals. Update it when it no longer feels aligned. This is your journey. Your board should grow with you. You don't need permission to dream bigger or aim higher. A vision board simply helps you remember, on the days when it's hard, that your future is still yours to create.

## DIY Projects: Crafting Confidence and Comfort

Think about sitting down with a handful of colorful materials–threads, fabric, beads, or even some calming essential oils. Use these materials in whatever way feels good to you. You're not just making something cute. You're building confidence with every stitch, swirl, or brushstroke. DIY projects aren't just crafts. They're quiet acts of self-expression, self-trust, and self-celebration.

There's something powerful about creating something with your own hands. Whether you're making a friendship bracelet, designing your room decor, or mixing up a homemade sugar scrub, you're proving to yourself that *you can do this.* That sense of accomplishment? It sticks with you long after the paint dries or the bracelet is tied. Every finished piece becomes a reminder of your creativity, your patience, and your ability to follow through.

DIY is more than a hobby, it's an invitation to get curious and try new things. No one's asking you to be perfect. You just need to show up. Try painting a tote bag with your favorite quote or tie-dyeing an old hoodie into something fresh and new. Create a set of calming bath salts with lavender and chamomile, or make a candle that smells like your favorite season. These projects are about taking ownership of your space, your time, and how you care for yourself.

And the best part? You don't have to keep it all to yourself. Invite a few friends over for a chill DIY night. Put on a playlist, spread out your materials, and work together to create something. You'll be surprised how creativity brings people closer. Or share your work online. It's not about likes, it's about connection. Finding people who say, "I love that," or "I tried this too," reminds you that you're not alone in your journey.

DIY projects remind you of what's possible when you trust yourself. They help you slow down, enjoy the moment, and take pride in what you create. Whether it's a bracelet, a candle, or a little reminder taped to your wall, every handmade piece is a quiet kind of power. A whisper that says, "I did this. And I can do so much more."

## Exploring New Hobbies and Interests

Let's say you're stepping into a pottery class for the first time, and the cool clay beneath your hands is ready to be shaped into something beautiful. Trying new hobbies like this can be a game-changer for your self-confidence and personal growth. The aim is to step out of your comfort zone and discover the hidden talents and interests you never knew you had. Each new activity you try opens the door to a different part of yourself, revealing passions and skills that can boost your self-esteem and broaden your horizons. Whether it's the satisfaction of forming a perfect bowl on the wheel or capturing the perfect shot during a photography walk, these experiences enrich your life and build diverse skill sets that you carry forward.

Consider learning a musical instrument. The initial challenge might be daunting, but with each note you master, you unlock a new way to express yourself. Music becomes a language through which you communicate emotions and ideas, and each practice session is a step toward mastering this new form of expression. Photography walks offer another avenue for creativity. With a camera in hand, you see the world through a different lens, learning to appreciate the beauty in everyday moments. Each click is a snapshot of your perspective, a way to share how you see the world with others. Engaging in these hobbies not only hones your skills but also enriches your self-awareness and appreciation for the world around you.

Curiosity fuels self-love by driving you to explore and learn. It's the engine behind personal growth, encouraging you to ask questions and seek new experiences. It says, "I believe in myself enough to try." When you're curious, you open your mind to possibilities, fostering a love for learning that extends beyond the classroom. This curiosity can lead you to join local art clubs or online interest groups, connecting you with others who share your passions. These communities provide a sense of belonging and support, where you can share your progress, gain feedback, and find motivation. The connections and friendships you form along the way are as meaningful as the hobbies themselves. Through these shared experiences, you grow not just in skills but also in confidence and self-assurance.

# Chapter Nine

# Embracing Your Unique Self

"My Identity Is a Superpower – Not an Obstacle"
America Ferrera

Here's a moment you might recognize: you're standing in front of your closet, holding an outfit your friends all think is cool, but it just doesn't feel like you. You try it on anyway, hoping it helps you fit in, but the discomfort is instant. It's like putting on someone else's skin. That uneasy feeling? It's your inner voice reminding you of who you are. When you're living out of sync with your values, it shows up as self-doubt, disconnection, and sometimes even frustration. Your values are like a compass, guiding you toward what feels right for *you*, not what looks right for everyone else.

Values aren't just words, they're the foundation of your identity. They shape how you treat others, what you believe in, and the goals you chase. If honesty is one of your core values, you might choose to speak up even when it's hard. If kindness drives you, your actions will reflect empathy and care. These invisible drivers help you make decisions that align with who you are at your core, which builds confidence and clarity in the long run.

When you live by your values, you stop second-guessing yourself to please others and start making choices that feel solid and real.

To figure out what matters most to you, try a value-sorting activity. Write down words like creativity, loyalty, freedom, or justice–whatever speaks to you. Then, rank them. Which ones feel essential? Which ones could you let go of? You might be surprised at what rises to the top. You can also try guided tools, such as values worksheets (Therapist Aid has a great one), that walk you through the process. Once you know your values, decisions get easier, and living authentically becomes something you *do* rather than something you *hope for.*

Authenticity means being your true self, not a version crafted to impress or blend in. It's about owning your truth–your quirks, your beliefs, your voice. And while this can feel risky, especially in a world that pressures you to conform, the reward is huge: absolute confidence and real connections. When you're authentic, the friendships you build are stronger, the goals you pursue are yours, and the life you're creating feels right.

Of course, being yourself isn't always easy. There will be times when people question your choices or expect you to go along with something that doesn't align with your values. That's where confidence comes in, not the loud kind, but the quiet, steady kind that reminds you, "I know who I am, and that's enough."

The friend group of 15-year-old Ava started copying a particular influencer's look–the same makeup, same captions, same attitude. But Ava just wasn't feeling it. She loved her natural style and the cozy, comfy aesthetic she'd curated. Instead of changing herself to fit in, she stayed true to what made her feel comfortable. And guess what? A few months later, other girls started asking Ava about her look and where she got her oversized sweaters. Her authenticity made her magnetic, and it helped her find people who genuinely liked her for *who she was.*

To stay rooted in your identity, surround yourself with people who support your individuality. Keep a journal to track your wins, moments when you stood by your values and said "no" to something that didn't feel right. Reflecting on these moments helps build the confidence to keep doing it. And remember: your identity is not something to hide or fix, it's your greatest asset. Own it, protect it, and let it shine.

## Exercise: Discovering Your Core Values

Find a quiet space where you can reflect without distractions, and grab your journal or a blank piece of paper. Start by thinking about a time when you felt genuinely proud of yourself or deeply fulfilled. Maybe it was when you stood up for a friend, finished a challenging project, or showed up fully as yourself. What values were you honoring in that moment? Write them down. Now, think about a time when you felt off, conflicted, or uncomfortable. What was happening? Were your values being pushed aside or ignored by yourself or by others? Jot those down, too.

With both lists in front of you, look for patterns. What keeps showing up? Begin ranking these values, placing the ones that feel most important at the top. These are your non-negotiables, the values that guide your everyday choices and help you feel grounded. Other values might still matter, but their importance may shift depending on the situation. That's okay. This exercise is about getting honest with yourself, not creating a perfect list.

Revisit your values often. As you grow, your priorities might change, and that's part of living authentically. Keep this list somewhere you can come back to when you're making tough decisions or need a reminder of what matters most.

Learning what you stand for is a decisive step toward embracing your true self. When you know your values, you stop fitting into molds that were never made for you. Instead, you move through the world with purpose, confidence, and clarity. Let your values be your compass, and trust that you're exactly who you're meant to be.

## Gender and Sexuality: Embracing Your True Self

Stand in front of a mirror, not just to check your hair or outfit, but to *see* yourself. Not the version of you that others expect to see. Not what you've been told to be. But who you are. That's what exploring your gender identity and sexuality is about. It's peeling back the layers of outside noise so you can connect with what's true for *you.*

Gender identity is how you feel inside, whether that's male, female, both, neither, or somewhere in between. It's not always the same as the sex you were assigned at birth. Sexuality, on the other hand, is about who you're attracted to emotionally, romantically, or physically. This might be straight, gay, bi, pan, ace, or something else entirely. These terms are all part of a much broader and more fluid spectrum than many people realize.

Think of gender and sexuality like a paint palette, not just black and white, but filled with endless colors, shades, and combinations. It's about finding the ones that reflect who you are. And it's okay if your understanding of yourself shifts over time. That's not confusion; it's growth.

Self-exploration plays a significant role in this journey. Try some reflective journaling with questions like, "When do I feel most like myself?" or "What am I scared to say out loud?" Write without editing your words. Let your truth rise to the surface, no pressure, no rules, just space to be honest with yourself. Supportive communities make a huge difference. Whether it's an LGBTQ+ club at school, a Discord server, or a group on TikTok or Reddit, connecting with others who "get it" can be life-changing. These spaces help you feel seen, heard, and not alone.

15-year-old Maya always knew she didn't feel entirely comfortable calling herself straight, but she couldn't quite name what she felt. At first, she kept quiet, unsure if anyone would understand. Then, she joined an online group where teens shared their experiences with being pansexual. Reading their stories felt like turning on a light inside her. Slowly, she began to explore what it meant and realized it was a good fit. It took some time before her mom understood the difference between pansexual and bisexual, but they were able to speak openly about it, and this helped Maya even more. Now, she feels proud of who she is and more confident about expressing it.

17-year-old Madison never quite felt at ease with being called a "girl" the way others seemed to. She tried to go along with what was expected, dressing a certain way, responding to "pretty girl" compliments, but something always felt off. It wasn't until she met another teen who identified as nonbinary at a summer art program that things began to click. They had long conversations about gender being a spectrum, not a fixed category. For the first time, Madison felt safe to question things. She started experimenting with pronouns, with her clothes, with how she introduced herself. It didn't all happen overnight, but slowly, Madison began to feel more like Madison. That shift, from hiding to exploring, meant everything.

Your gender and sexuality are parts of who you are, but they don't define your worth. There is no deadline to figure it all out. There is no rulebook to follow. What matters most is giving yourself permission to explore, question, and change. You don't owe anyone an explanation, and you're not "too much" or "not enough" of anything in between. You are just right as you are.

## Standing Out with Pride and Confidence

Have you walked into a room filled with people, where each person has their unique style, energy, and presence? The ones who stand out aren't necessarily the loudest or the most dramatic. They're the ones who own who they are. They show up confidently without pretending to be someone they're not. That's what standing out means: Being so rooted in your truth that you don't need to seek approval to shine. When you embrace your individuality, you create room for real growth. People start to see your strengths, perspective, and creativity. New friendships form. Opportunities open up. It is more powerful to be real on purpose than it is to be different on purpose.

Take school projects, for example. When you bring your ideas to a group assignment instead of copying what everyone else is doing, the result often stands out. That's precisely what happened to 14-year-old Brooklyn. In a science presentation, her group wanted to keep it simple, but Leila suggested adding storytelling and visuals to explain their topic in a way everyone could relate to. Her idea made the project more engaging and more memorable. She didn't push for attention. She just brought her personality and vision into it. That's what it means to stand out by being yourself.

The way you dress can also be a vibrant expression of who you are. Your clothes aren't just fabric; they are statements. Every pattern, color, or accessory is an opportunity to show the world a part of you. Maybe you wear your favorite band tee because music is your thing, or a bright scarf that always puts you in a good mood. When you dress for yourself, not for likes or compliments, you show confidence without having to say a word. You're saying, "This is me, and I like her."

Of course, standing out isn't always easy. It can bring up fears like, "What if they laugh?" or "What if I don't fit in?" That's totally normal. But don't let those fears make decisions for you. When Taylor was 13, she started wearing clothes that didn't match her school's typical trends–like big earrings and vintage jeans and some people gave her strange looks at first. But she kept showing up as herself, and eventually, others started complimenting her style or asking where she shopped. Confidence is contagious. And it begins with positive self-talk. When doubt creeps in, remind yourself, "I have the right to take up space," or "My style reflects my strength."

And look around at the women who inspire you. Amanda Gorman didn't wait to be older or more experienced to speak her truth–she just did it, and the world listened. Megan Rapinoe didn't tone herself down for anyone–she used her platform to fight for what mattered. These women didn't blend in. They stood tall in their truth and let the world adjust to them. That's power. They weren't fearless. They were courageous. There's a difference. Courage means doing it even when you're nervous. That's what you're building every time you choose to be yourself instead of what you think is expected of you.

So, as we wrap up this chapter, here's your reminder: standing out doesn't mean putting on a show. It means showing up. It means choosing authenticity over approval and letting your unique light be seen. Whether you're bold or quiet, artsy or analytical, funny or serious–whatever your vibe, that's your power. Own it.

CHAPTER TEN

# Personal Growth and Self-Improvement

"I found that ultimately if you truly pour your heart into what you believe in, even if it makes you vulnerable, amazing things can and will happen."
Emma Watson

## The SMART method

Close your eyes and visualize yourself standing at the edge of a vast, open field. The air is full of possibility. That space in front of you? It's your potential: your dreams, your goals, your future. It's exciting, but it can also feel overwhelming. Where do you even begin? That's where goal setting comes in. Setting goals is like planting seeds in that field. Each one gives you direction, purpose, and something tangible to work toward. Instead of getting lost in all the "what ifs," you start creating a path forward–one clear step at a time.

One of the first things to learn is the difference between short-term and long-term goals. Short-term goals are your daily and weekly wins, the little things that build momentum and give you confidence. Long-term goals are your bigger dreams. Maybe it's graduating with top grades, applying to a specific college, or mastering a skill you've always admired in others. They take time, but give you something powerful to aim for. Short-term goals keep you moving. Long-term goals keep you focused on what matters to you.

To ensure your goals are practical, use the SMART method. That means setting goals that are:

- **Specific:** What exactly do you want to do?
- **Measurable:** How will you know you're making progress?
- **Achievable:** Is this goal realistic right now?
- **Relevant:** Does this goal matter to you?
- **Time-bound:** When will you get it done by?

Let's say you want to improve your math grade. Instead of saying, "I want to get better at math," try: "I want to raise my math grade by 10% in the next three months by going to tutoring every week and practicing three times a week at home." That's a SMART goal, and you've got a real plan.

Big goals can feel like too much all at once, but breaking them into smaller tasks makes them doable. It's like building a LEGO set, you don't snap it all together in one move. You follow the steps, and each step you take is worth celebrating. Taking steps builds confidence and reminds you that you're making progress, even at moments when it doesn't feel like you are.

Visual tools, such as goal trackers, charts, or digital planners, can also be helpful. Whether it's a chart on your wall or a tracker app on your phone, seeing your progress every day can boost your motivation and keep you on track.

Growth takes time. Progress isn't always linear; it doesn't have to follow a set path where one step naturally comes after the other. Sometimes it's more like a rollercoaster with twists and turns. But every step forward, big or small, is a reminder that you are capable, committed, and becoming more of the person you want to be.

## The Fear of Failure: Turning Setbacks into Strengths

Imagine standing on the edge of a diving board, staring down at the water. Your heart races, and a voice in your head whispers, "What if I mess up?" That's fear of failure–a feeling most of us know well. But what if failure wasn't something to avoid but something to learn from? What if each setback was just a step toward something greater?

Fear of failure can feel huge, like it's holding you back from even trying. But reframing it as part of the learning process changes everything. Oprah Winfrey was told she wasn't fit for TV. Serena Williams reminds us that comebacks are what define a champion. They didn't let failure stop them, instead, they used it to fuel their growth.

Start by reflecting on mistakes instead of burying them. Keep a small "fail journal" and write down what happened, how you felt, and what you learned. Over time, you'll see patterns and growth. It's not about feeling ashamed, it's about getting curious. Another helpful tool? A personal SWOT analysis. That means thinking about your Strengths, Weaknesses, Opportunities, and Threats. It's a simple way to figure out where you are and what you do next. There is a SWOT exercise in the comprehensive workbook with further explanation.

One of the most empowering things you can do is name your fears. What are you terrified of? Messing up in front of others? Looking dumb? Once you understand the fear, you can begin to break it down. Are you scared of public speaking? Start small. Practice in front of your mirror. Then, a friend. Then a small group. Every step makes it a little less scary.

Mistakes don't define you; they grow you. Reflect on what happened. Decide on what you would do differently next time. This is how you build resilience: an honest look at one setback at a time. And don't forget to ask for help. Talk to a mentor or a trusted adult. Their feedback might just be the boost you need to keep going.

Let's take 15-year-old Hailey. She applied to join her school's student council and didn't get in. She felt embarrassed and convinced herself she wasn't leadership material. But after journaling about what happened, she realized she hadn't practiced for the interview questions. Instead of quitting, she asked a teacher for help and practiced with a friend for the following year. When the next round came, she was ready–and she got in. Hailey's story is a reminder: failure hurts, but it also teaches us valuable lessons. It builds the kind of confidence that only comes from trying again.

I've been there, too. In one of my jobs, a small mistake, even one that's only 0.04%, can feel like the end of the world. I used to spiral whenever I got that kind of feedback, thinking I wasn't good enough. However, over time, I learned to breathe, take in the input, and use the feedback to grow. Now, I view making mistakes as opportunities rather than personal attacks. I learned to "fail forward." I take the lesson, and keep going. That shift didn't happen overnight. But I got myself there with patience and self-compassion.

## Building Determination: Staying the Course

Look at determination as standing on a track, the finish line far off in the distance. Each step forward feels heavy, but you keep going. That's what determination looks like. It's not flashy or loud, it's quiet persistence. It's the fuel that keeps you moving when motivation disappears, when things get boring, and when you want to quit but don't. Determination is what separates wishful thinking from real progress. It gets you through late-night study sessions, early-morning practices, and uncomfortable moments when things feel uncertain. The connection between determination and success isn't random–it's cause and effect. Every accomplishment has determination at its core.

Determination doesn't magically appear. You build it, one choice at a time. Start by creating a personal mantra or a quote that resonates with you. Something short, intense, and easy to repeat. "I don't stop when I'm tired,

I stop when I'm done," or "I've done hard things before, and I'll do this too." Say it every morning. Say it when you want to give up. Say it until it becomes part of how you think.

Another way to stay on course? Set an intention for the day. Just one. It could be finishing your math homework or starting a tough conversation. A daily intention gives your brain direction. It says, "Here's what we're doing today," and it keeps you focused on your bigger goal, even when life feels messy.

But let's be honest: determination doesn't come easy. Procrastination and self-doubt will show up. You'll think, "I'll do it later," or "What if I'm not good enough?" These are distractions dressed up as logic. The trick is to spot your traps. Maybe you delay things because you're scared it won't be perfect. Perhaps you should wait because the task feels too big. Either way, break it down. Do one part. Set a timer. Just start. Momentum is everything.

Self-doubt is tougher. It whispers that you're not smart enough, strong enough, or talented enough. That's when you fight back with facts. Keep a list of your wins, big or small. A good grade. A compliment from a teacher. A moment when you stood up for yourself. Re-read it when your confidence shakes. And don't isolate, but talk to someone who believes in you. This could be a friend, mentor, parent, or coach. Let their belief in you hold you steady until you remember your own.

I want to tell you about 15-year-old Sienna. She wanted to audition for the school's theater production. She loved acting, but the thought of rejection paralyzed her. Every day, she told herself she wasn't good enough. But instead of giving in, she started practicing one line daily in front of the mirror. Then to her little sister. Then to a friend. Slowly, the fear shrank. She auditioned. She didn't get the lead, but she landed a role, and now she is helping other girls prep for next semester's show. Sienna's secret? She didn't wait to stop being scared. She chose to keep going anyway.

Determination isn't about being fearless. It's about choosing to stay in the game. Every day you show up is a win. Every time you don't quit, you get stronger. You don't need to sprint to the finish line. Just keep walking, one step at a time.

## The Growth Mindset: Embracing Change and Challenge

Have you ever wanted to start something new? Maybe it's your first piano lesson, your first debate team meeting, or walking into a new school. Your stomach flips. You feel that nervous energy. And right there, in that very moment, you have a choice: to shut down or to lean in. The choice to do it despite the nerves is the essence of a growth mindset.

A growth mindset is the belief that your abilities, intelligence, and talents aren't fixed but that they can grow. With effort, curiosity, and the willingness to try again (and again), you can improve at anything. Challenges stop feeling like roadblocks and start looking like opportunities. This mindset turns "I'm not good at this" into "I'm not good at this *yet.*" It gives you the courage to try, fail, learn, and try again.

Now, let's contrast that with a fixed mindset. That voice says, "You're just not a math person," or "You'll never be as talented as her." Thoughts like this convince you that mistakes are proof you're not good enough. However, here's what the Chinese say: teens with a growth mindset experience *less stress and fewer mental health issues* (and that's backed by real research). Why? Because they see setbacks as part of the process, not proof that they should give up.

So, how do you shift into a growth mindset? Start by changing the way you look at challenges. Instead of dreading a tough test or a new class, try seeing it as a way to stretch your brain. It's not about acing it the first time, it's about learning something new. And yes, gratitude helps here, too. Keep a journal where you note one thing you learned each week, even if it came from messing up: gratitude + reflection = growth.

Try this: the next time you make a mistake, instead of saying, "Ugh, I'm terrible at this," say, "Okay, what can I learn from this?" It might feel cheesy at first, but it works. Over time, this kind of reframing becomes your automatic response.

Grace, a 14-year-old, used to dread science class. Every test made her anxious, and every mistake felt like proof she wasn't smart enough. However, Grace decided to approach things differently after learning about the growth mindset. She started asking more questions, even when she was nervous. She reviewed her incorrect answers and identified where she had gone wrong. Her grades slowly improved, but more importantly, so did her confidence. She went from saying, "I hate science," to "I'm still figuring it out." That's the power of mindset.

You can also set personal "stretch goals" that push you just beyond what's comfortable. Try something new, a coding class, an improv club, or martial arts. These experiences build more than skill; they build *you* up. They teach you how to keep going when things get tough. And creativity plays a role, too. Writing, painting, or doing DIY projects can help you explore new ways of thinking and problem-solving.

Once you begin living with a growth mindset, change becomes something to lean into, instead of something to run from. You get curious. You take risks. You stop seeing failure as something to fear and start seeing it as a stepping stone forward. Your brain is powerful. So is your mindset. And the truth is: you get to choose which one you feed. Choose growth, girl. I believe in you.

## Chapter Eleven

# Mindfulness and Self-Care Rituals

"Your mental health should be your priority. Don't let anyone make you feel guilty for taking care of yourself."
Lili Reinhart

Visualize this: you're walking through a crowded school hallway. Lockers bang shut, friends are laughing loudly, and conversations swirl around you. But, right in the middle of that chaos, you're able to pause. You take a breath. And just for a moment, everything quiets. That's the silent strength of mindfulness. It's not about escaping the chaos but learning how to be present within it.

Mindfulness means being fully present, right there, right now, without judging yourself or your thoughts. It's the art of noticing. Though rooted in ancient meditation practices, mindfulness isn't only for yoga classes or quiet corners. It can become an integral part of your everyday life, helping you navigate stress, overwhelm, and uncertainty with clarity and calm.

When you focus on what's happening in the present instead of replaying something awkward that occurred last week or stressing over a test tomorrow, your anxiety starts to loosen its grip. Mindfulness helps quiet that inner storm. It doesn't magically make problems disappear, but it gives you the strength and space to face them with more clarity and calm.

When you're caught in a spiral of worry or distracted by a hundred thoughts at once, mindfulness brings you back to the present moment. One simple way you can ground yourself is to engage your senses. Try this grounding technique:

- Notice **five** things you can see
- **Four** things you can touch
- **Three** things you can hear
- **Two** things you can smell
- **One** thing you can taste

It may seem insignificant, but these small check-ins have a profound impact. They shift your focus away from anxious loops and anchor you in the now. You're not trying to empty your mind. You're just watching your thoughts pass through like clouds without chasing or judging them.

The best part? You don't need a meditation cushion or a quiet room to practice. Mindfulness fits into real life. Try *deep breathing* when you're overwhelmed: slowly inhale through your nose, pause, and then exhale through your mouth. Let your body settle. Or try *mindful eating*. Instead of rushing through lunch, slow down. Notice the textures, colors, and taste of your food. Be present with your meal.

Try *mindful walking*. On your way to class or while walking the dog, focus on how your feet feel as they touch the ground. Notice the rhythm of your steps, the sounds around you, and how the air feels. Or do a *body scan* before bed, paying attention to each part of your body, starting from your toes and working your way up to the top of your head, softening any tension as you go. These quick resets don't just feel good, they teach your brain to stay calm and present. These tiny shifts in awareness create a significant ripple effect. They bring your mind and body into sync and build emotional resilience over time.

Let's be honest: when you first try mindfulness, your brain might be all over the place. That's *normal*. The goal isn't to "empty your mind" or "do it perfectly." The goal is to show up, observe what's happening, and return to the moment when your mind drifts. That *is* the practice. That's also where self-awareness grows. The more you practice, the more naturally it comes until mindfulness becomes a quiet kind of power that follows you everywhere.

## Mindful Breathing: Finding Calm in Chaos

Let's try it out: taking a slow, deep breath that fills your lungs and gently settles your thoughts. Mindful breathing isn't just about inhaling and exhaling, it's one of the quickest and most powerful ways to calm your mind and body. When you focus on your breath, you're signaling to your nervous system that it's safe to relax. This simple practice activates the parasympathetic nervous system, the part of your body responsible for rest and recovery, and slows your heart rate, lowers blood pressure, and reduces the stress hormone cortisol. It's like flipping a physical switch from chaos to calm.

Breathing mindfully can quickly ground you when anxiety creeps in. Whether you're overwhelmed by schoolwork, frozen with test-day nerves, or feeling emotionally off-balance, focused breathing helps anchor you in the present. Regular practice doesn't just ease stress, it improves your concentration and emotional regulation. The more often you pause to breathe with intention, the easier it becomes to stay centered when life throws curveballs. It's a quiet, powerful way to hit reset, especially when your mind is racing and you need to refocus.

There are several simple techniques worth exploring. Diaphragmatic breathing, where you breathe deeply into your belly instead of your chest, helps maximize oxygen intake and encourages full-body relaxation. Box breathing–inhale, hold, exhale, hold, each for a count of four–is especially helpful in stressful moments when your thoughts are spinning. Alternate nostril breathing is a traditional practice that promotes calmness and balance. The 4-7-8 technique, which involves inhaling for four counts, holding for seven, and exhaling for eight, is particularly effective in easing anxiety and improving focus. Try them out and see what works best for you.

13-year-old Alina used to get so anxious before volleyball games that her hands would shake and her thoughts would spiral out of control. Her coach taught her to pause and do four slow rounds of 4-7-8 breathing before warm-ups. Now, it's her go-to routine before big games or tests. "It's like my brain gets quiet," she told her sister. "I feel more in control, even when I'm nervous." That's the power of the breath: it gives you a tool to calm your body, steady your mind, and show up as your best self.

I also use a version of the 4-7-8 breathing technique. These days, I don't even count unless I'm really anxious. I just make sure my exhale is longer than my inhale. I do it every day, often without thinking about it. It helps me reset in just a few breaths, whether I'm in a stressful meeting or just feeling off. Find your version, and make it yours.

## Morning Rituals: Starting Your Day with Intention

You know that soft glow of morning light slipping through your curtains? It's a new day, a clean page, and how you begin it matters more than you think. Morning rituals are like pressing "start" on your day with purpose. Instead of rushing into the chaos, a simple, intentional routine grounds you and sets a calm, focused tone. It's not about packing your morning with tasks, it's about choosing how you want to show up. Just like an intense opening scene in a movie, a solid start gives you energy and direction for everything that follows.

One of the simplest ways to shift into a mindful morning is by starting with gratitude. Before you even get out of bed, think of three things you're thankful for. Maybe it's your cozy blanket, the sound of birds outside, or a message from a friend that made you smile yesterday. Gratitude gently nudges your brain toward the positive and helps you focus on what's already good. From there, visualization can take things a step further. Close your eyes and picture your day: walking into school with confidence, tackling your to-do list with focus, and ending the day feeling proud of how you showed up. This kind of mental rehearsal prepares your brain to face challenges with clarity and calm.

Adding just a few intentional moments to your morning can make a huge difference. It might be stretching for five minutes while listening to music that lifts your mood. It might be sipping tea while journaling a quick note about how you're feeling–these small acts of self-care build emotional momentum. You don't need an elaborate routine; you need one that works for *you.*

16-year-old Ella used to feel like she was in survival mode every morning. With the rushing, skipping breakfast, scrolling through social media, and starting her day frazzled. Everything changed when her aunt talked to her about her stress levels. Ella decided to create a five-minute morning ritual. Now, she starts her day with three deep breaths, writes down one intention in her notebook, and makes time for a real breakfast. She told her aunt that she started feeling more in control. Even when the rest of the day felt busy, she knew she started it with something that was just for her.

That's the power of a mindful morning. It reminds you that your day belongs to you. You don't have to be perfect, and your routine doesn't have to be fancy. What matters is showing up for yourself first thing every day.

## Guided Imagery: Visualizing Your Best Self

Close your eyes for a moment and imagine standing in a place where you feel calm, confident, and entirely at ease. Maybe you're walking along a quiet beach, or you're confidently presenting in front of your class, feeling strong and collected. This type of visualization is the heart of guided imagery; a mental technique that lets your imagination become a tool for emotional balance and inner strength. It's more than daydreaming. It's a powerful way to shift your mindset, boost your confidence, and calm your nerves when life feels overwhelming.

Guided imagery works by creating vivid mental pictures that shape how you think and feel. When you imagine yourself succeeding, your brain starts to believe it's possible. That belief builds confidence and motivation. Visualizing positive outcomes, such as acing a test, speaking clearly during a presentation, or simply feeling calm in a stressful situation, helps prepare your mind to handle those real-life moments with greater ease. It's like rehearsing success until it feels natural.

There's science behind why this works. Visualization helps your brain form mental pathways that support the creation of new habits. Like practicing a physical skill, it can help lower stress levels, soothe anxiety, and aid in emotional reset. Think of it as a peaceful mental retreat you can visit whenever you need a break. Some teens even use guided imagery to help them fall asleep–visualizing soft waves, quiet forests, or floating among stars to settle their thoughts and relax their bodies.

To try it out, find a quiet space and sit or lie down comfortably. Close your eyes and take a few deep breaths. Then, build our mental scene. What do you see? Hear? Smell? Maybe you're at your favorite spot in nature or standing confidently in a moment you've been nervous about. Let your imagination paint every detail. As you visualize, add affirmations that match the scene: "I am safe and calm," "I trust myself," or "I can handle this." The more senses and emotions you bring to the experience, the more powerful the effect will be.

Natalie, a 15-year-old, used to get anxious before baseball games. Her coach taught her to visualize the entire match in her mind, from warm-ups to getting a home run. She started practicing this the night before each game. At first, it felt bizarre, but then it began to work. She'd already seen herself succeed, so when the game started, she was less nervous. Guided imagery became her pre-game ritual, and it helped her play with more focus and confidence.

This simple tool is always available to you. Whether you're preparing for a challenge, trying to manage stress, or just need a mental reset, guided imagery can support you from the inside out. Let your mind create the path forward, and trust that you already have everything you need to walk it.

## Yoga and Meditation: Finding Inner Peace

Let's say you're standing tall in your room, feet firmly planted, shoulders relaxed, eyes closed. You're not rushing to do anything or be anyone. You're just there, still and ready, feeling your breath and your body. That's what yoga invites you to do: slow down, tune in, and reconnect with yourself. Yoga is about more than flexibility or cool poses; it's a way to calm your mind, strengthen your body, and build emotional resilience. Rooted in ancient traditions, yoga is about unity: the connection between body, mind, and spirit. And when paired with meditation, it becomes a powerful practice for finding peace, especially when life feels chaotic or overwhelming.

If you're new to yoga, don't worry about doing it perfectly. Start simple. A pose like a mountain pose–where you stand tall, feet hip-width apart, arms relaxed at your sides–is excellent for grounding yourself. You can also try a child's pose, where you kneel, sit back on your heels, and stretch your arms forward with your forehead resting on the floor. It's a gentle, comforting position that gives you a moment to relax. These small movements can help release tension and quiet your thoughts. With practice, you can build on these poses, adding more as your comfort and confidence grow. The goal isn't to "perform" yoga, it's to feel your breath, notice your body, and come home to yourself.

Meditation offers a similar kind of reset but focuses more on stillness. One type, called mindfulness meditation, teaches you to sit quietly and simply notice what's happening in your body and mind, without judgment. It's as simple as breathing in, breathing out, and being okay with whatever comes up. Another option is loving-kindness meditation, where you repeat phrases like "May I be safe. May I be happy. May I be well," and then extend those wishes to others–friends, family, even people with whom you struggle. It might sound soft, but it builds strength. Over time, these practices can help you stay calm under pressure and respond to challenges with clarity and compassion.

You don't need a yoga mat or a fancy setup to begin. All you need is a quiet space, a corner of your room, a spot by your window, even your bed. Try setting aside five minutes a day. You could stretch in the morning to wake up your body or sit in quiet meditation before bed to let go of the day. You can also explore free online resources, like guided meditations on YouTube or beginner yoga flows on apps. What matters most is consistency, not perfection.

14-year-old Addison started doing ten minutes of yoga every morning after her mom noticed how anxious she was before school. Her mom had recently started doing yoga, and she taught Addison a couple of poses she could do. Addison then started following a short beginner video online and added a two-minute breathing meditation afterward. After a few weeks, she told her mom she felt much better in the morning. It felt like she started the day on her terms. That's what is most important: making space to care for yourself in small, intentional ways.

Yoga and meditation don't have to be intimidating or complicated. They're tools you can use anytime, anywhere, to check in with yourself. And you get to create calm from the inside out. The more you practice, the more you'll notice how these moments of peace stay with you, not just on the mat or in silence, but in the middle of your day when you need them most.

## The Power of Pause: Taking Breaks for Mental Health

Have you ever been at your desk, totally focused on a project, hours slipping by without you even noticing? While being in the zone can feel productive, going too long without a break can have the opposite effect. Your brain gets tired, your concentration drops, and suddenly everything feels harder to accomplish. Taking breaks isn't lazy, it's smart. Think of it like charging your phone. Even the most powerful devices need to pause and plug in. Your mind works the same way. A short break gives your brain space to reset, and sometimes, that's precisely when the best ideas come through–when you're not forcing them.

One helpful strategy is the Pomodoro Technique. You work for 25 minutes, then take a five-minute break. It sounds simple, but it's surprisingly effective. During those breaks, try doing something that recharges your energy. Maybe it's stepping outside for a quick breath of fresh air, stretching your legs, or closing your eyes for a few deep breaths. A short walk or a quick sketch session can reset your mind in just a few minutes. When you start feeling foggy, easily distracted, or frustrated, that's a sign your brain needs a reset. Listen to those signals and allow yourself to step back.

Screens make it even trickier. We're so used to staring at phones, laptops, and tablets that we forget how draining they can be. Taking regular breaks from tech, especially social media, can do wonders for your mental clarity. Try putting your phone down for just ten minutes and doing something offline, like journaling or flipping through a book. These quiet moments help your brain switch gears. And when you give your eyes and mind a break from blue light, you might also sleep better at night. Too much screen time, especially before bed, messes with your sleep, leaving you groggy the next day.

It's not just about physical rest. Taking a break from constant online pressure is also a kind of emotional reset. Social media can be overwhelming; the notifications, the pressure to stay connected, the endless scrolling. Stepping away, even briefly, can give you room to breathe. You might be surprised how much more present and focused you feel afterward. And you might also find you're better able to connect with the people around you, in real-time, without distractions. Breaks aren't just pauses; they're power moves that protect your energy and keep you going strong.

## Sleep Hygiene: Resting Your Mind and Body

Think of sleep as your superpower. It recharges your brain, resets your emotions, and helps you function at your best. When you get quality sleep, everything feels easier. You focus better, remember more, manage your mood, and stay motivated. That's because sleep isn't just "rest". It's when your brain processes what you have experienced, stores memories, and helps you reset emotionally. Without enough sleep, your body and mind begin to fall behind.

Creating a healthy sleep routine is key, and it starts with consistency. Try to go to bed and wake up at the same time every day, even on weekends. This trains your body to follow a natural rhythm, making it easier to fall asleep and wake up feeling rested. You can create a wind-down routine that tells your brain it's time to relax. That might be putting on soft music, doing gentle stretches, journaling, or reading a few pages of a book. These rituals help you transition from the chaos of the day to a space where rest comes more easily.

One big sleep killer? Screens. The blue light from your phone, tablet, or laptop tricks your brain into staying alert, making it harder to fall asleep. Just scrolling through social media before bed can overstimulate your mind. I suggest powering down your devices at least an hour before sleep. You can also switch on night mode, use blue light filters, or wear blue-light-blocking glasses. But honestly, your best bet is to swap the scroll for something soothing, anything that helps you unplug from the noise and reconnect with calm.

Your bedroom matters too. Try to keep it calm, dark, and quiet. Use blackout curtains, play soft rain sounds, or use a calming scent like lavender to create a cozy, sleep-friendly space. The more your space supports rest, the easier it is for your body to relax and your brain to slow down.

I didn't take sleep seriously when I was a teen. I thought I was fine with 4-6 hours of sleep a night. I wanted to stay up late and squeeze in more time for everything else. Spoiler: that backfired. In my mid-twenties, I struggled with severe depression, and my sleep was awful. It took me forever to fall asleep, and when I did, it wasn't restful. Even after things got better, my sleep didn't. I'd lie there for hours, brain buzzing with anxiety. And then something changed. I gave meditation a shot, even though I once swore I'd never be "that person." But within a week, everything shifted. I fell asleep faster, slept deeper, and woke up without that horrible groggy fog. Now, I use breathing and visualization almost every night. It's not perfect, but it's powerful.

I learned something game-changing: our sleep works in cycles. One complete cycle is about 90 minutes. So, if you figure out when you need to wake up, you can count backward in 90-minute blocks to find out the best time to go to bed. I try to get around 7,5 hours, which is five complete cycles. In the darker months, I might need more; in summer, I need less. I usually spend the first few minutes in bed thinking of what I'm grateful for; then, I start visualizing something I want in my future. It is like falling asleep with purpose, and waking up with energy.

I know this might sound boring or something you'll "figure out later," but trust me: your brain, your body, and your mood all need good sleep. Try just one small change and see how it feels. You don't have to change everything overnight. That's not possible either. But, if you start now, your future self will really appreciate it.

CHAPTER TWELVE

# Actionable Steps to Self-Love

"The minute you learn to love yourself,
you won't want to be anyone else."
Rihanna

Let's say you wake up to a soft glow of morning light and feel a quiet calm settle over you. You take a deep breath, stretch, and remind yourself that this is a fresh start. This peace isn't just wishful thinking; it's the result of something powerful called daily self-love rituals. These small, steady acts are like watering your inner garden, helping confidence and calm take root in your everyday life.

Self-love rituals aren't about doing something big and dramatic. They're about showing up for yourself in small ways every single day. Starting your morning with affirmations can shift your whole mindset. Use statements like "I am worthy just as I am" or "I choose to be kind to myself today." Try to think about it like seeing a friend when you're looking in the mirror, not a critic. Those words become your emotional armor, helping you walk through the day with a little more strength. And in the evening? That's your time to wind down. Light a candle, do a few gentle stretches, or write down three things you're grateful for. These quiet moments help you release the stress you've carried and recharge your energy.

Adding these rituals to your day can enhance your mood and overall physical and emotional well-being. Take a mindful walk and notice what's around you, the way the leaves move, the sun's warmth on your skin, or the rhythm of your footsteps. Or start a simple skincare routine, not because you're trying to impress anyone, but because it feels good to care for yourself. Whether it's brushing your hair slowly or putting on your favorite lip balm, these small acts remind you that you're worth your time and attention.

Like anything that matters, self-love grows with consistency. You wouldn't expect a plant to thrive if you only watered it occasionally. Your self-love needs the same steady care. Stick a quote on your mirror. Set a reminder on your phone. Build little habits into your day that support how you want to feel. It's not about perfection, but it's about showing up for yourself repeatedly.

And here's the most important part: make it yours. What lights you up might not work for someone else, and that's perfectly okay. Maybe you feel most grounded when painting, baking, dancing around your room, or writing in a journal. Try different things until you find what feels right. Self-care isn't one-size-fits-all, it's a personal act of love. Listen to yourself. Trust what feels good. That's how you create a self-love ritual that sticks and reminds you every day that you are enough.

## Personalized Self-Care Plan

Creating a self-care plan is like designing a roadmap back to yourself. Don't look at it as adding more to your to-do list, but as making space for what helps you feel calm, strong, and connected. This plan is your personalized toolkit, filled with routines and rituals that lift you and help you stay grounded through life's highs and lows. This plan will be your compass when things get hectic.

Start by grabbing your journal or opening a blank page in your notes app. Divide your plan into three simple actions: **Morning Rituals**, **Evening Relaxation**, and **Weekly Treats**. Under each, write down the practices that feel good for you; there is no pressure, no rules, just note down what feels right. Your morning ritual could include stretching, listening to a favorite playlist, or saying three affirmations in the mirror. Your evening might involve lighting a candle, taking a few deep breaths, or writing down what you are grateful for. And your weekly treats? These little joys recharge you: a long walk, a face mask, time with a good book, or baking your favorite dessert.

As you build your list, consider how each action makes you feel. Energized? Relaxed? Centered? If something stops feeling good, change it. As this is your plan, it should grow with you. Self-care isn't about sticking to a perfect routine, but instead about tuning in and honoring what you need, even as that changes.

Keep your self-care plan visible–a page in your journal, on your wall, or saved on your phone–so you can return to it when life feels overwhelming. Let it be your reminder that showing up for yourself matters. You deserve time, care, and peace of mind. And the more you practice these rituals, the more natural they become. Your self-love deserves a place in your daily life. Not just every once in a while, but every day.

## Confidence Hacks for Everyday Life

Have you ever woken up feeling steady, calm, and totally in your power? Confidence doesn't come from being perfect. It grows from daily choices that remind you of your identity and capabilities. One surprisingly effective tool? Power posing. It might sound silly at first, but research shows that your body language can influence your feelings. Try this: stand tall in front of your mirror each morning with your feet firmly planted and hands on your hips like a superhero. Stretch your arms up high and hold for a few seconds. Breathe in deeply. This simple act tells your brain, "I'm strong. I've got this." And it works. You'll walk into your day a little taller and a little more sure of yourself.

Another confidence-boosting skill is maintaining eye contact. It's a quiet, powerful way to show presence and self-trust. Whether speaking in class, chatting with a teacher, or talking to a friend, meeting someone's gaze (even for a moment) sends a message to you and the other person that you're confident and engaged. If it feels awkward at first, start small. Practice with someone you trust. You'll find that holding eye contact helps you feel more grounded and makes others take you more seriously.

Try starting a confidence journal, a small notebook or a notes app where you track your wins. Every evening, write down something you did that day that made you feel brave or proud. It could be as simple as raising your hand in class, standing up for someone, or trying something new. Over time, this journal becomes your collection of proof that you're growing. Flipping through those pages on hard days can remind you just how strong you are.

Affirmations are another go-to tool. These short, positive statements help you shift your inner dialogue. Instead of focusing on doubt, you intentionally choose words that reflect your worth. Think: "I believe in myself." "I am growing stronger every day." "I have something important to offer." You can write your affirmations in your journal, say them aloud in the mirror, or create cards decorated with quotes and doodles. Tape them to your mirror, tuck them in your bag, or use them as bookmarks. Let them be daily reminders of who you're becoming.

Confidence is a skill, not something you're born with or without. You build it by showing up for yourself in small ways daily. And each time you do, you become more connected to your confidence. You don't need to be perfect or loud to be confident. You just have to keep building your trust in yourself, one pose, one sentence, one step at a time.

## Journaling Prompts for Self-Reflection

Do you have a favorite cozy spot? Sit there with a notebook open on your lap and a pen in hand. There's something comforting about writing your thoughts–no filters, no pressure, no judgment, just a chance to be honest with yourself. Journaling is like having a heart-to-heart with yourself. It's how you get to figure things out, celebrate what makes you amazing, and work through whatever's in your heart.

Start by thinking about what makes you strong. Maybe you are determined to keep trying, even when things get hard. Perhaps it's how you always notice when someone needs a kind word or how your creativity shows up in everything you do. When you write these things down, they are reminders of what's already powerful about you, and these notes are something you can return to when you need a confidence boost.

Think back to a time when you felt completely and effortlessly like yourself. Maybe it was when you were painting, laughing with your best friend, or walking outside with music in your ears and no one telling you who you were. Remember how free that felt, how real. Writing about those moments helps you understand what brings you joy and shows you how to stay connected to the version of yourself that feels the most true.

It's also worth taking a moment to recognize the things you love about yourself. Not just the things others compliment you on, but the things that make you proud. Maybe it's your courage, curiosity, or how you always try to see the good in people. Listing those qualities can shift your mindset and remind you that you don't need to change to be worthy of love. You are already worthy as you are.

And when you think about how far you've come, you might surprise yourself. Maybe there was a time you stood up for someone, stayed calm under pressure, or finished something you thought you couldn't. Write about how that felt, what you learned, and how you grew. Those memories aren't just wins; they're proof that you're becoming stronger and more sure of yourself with every challenge you face.

Journaling isn't about writing perfect words or having everything figured out. It's about showing up for yourself, one page at a time. The more you write, the more you uncover who you are and who you're becoming. And being with your thoughts in those quiet moments, you'll find clarity, comfort, and a growing sense of self-love.

## The Self-Love Challenge: 30 Days to a Better You

If you want to, you can wake up each morning with a purpose, knowing that that day holds a small, meaningful task designed to nurture your self-love. Starting your days like this is the essence of the self-love challenge–a 30-day journey that offers a new opportunity for reflection and growth each day. The concept is simple yet profound: dedicating a month to intentional self-care and introspection can transform how you see yourself. It's not about grand gestures but setting intentions that align with who you are and aspire to be. You'll find the complete 30-Day Self-Love Challenge in your free mini-workbook. Please don't forget to download it by scanning the QR code in the beginning of the book.

Your self-love journey begins with a decision. Ask yourself why self-love matters to you right now. Maybe you want to feel more confident. Perhaps you're tired of comparing yourself to everyone else. Or do you want to feel at ease in your own skin? Whatever it is, hold onto that reason. Let it guide you through the next 30 days like a bit of light you can always return to.

Some days are about reflection. Other days invite you to unplug and be fully present, like when you take a break from social media and step back into your own life, without filters and likes, but just you. One day, you'll treat yourself to something you love just because it brings you joy. You will write a love letter to yourself. Tell yourself what makes you special–your kindness, creativity, and strength. It might feel awkward at first, but don't skip it. This letter becomes something powerful you can return to when you forget how amazing you are. And on the final day, you'll look back at the journey. You'll see how much you've grown and how much more connected you feel to who you truly are.

You don't have to do this alone. Sharing the challenge with a friend or creating a little group can make it even more meaningful. You can cheer each other on, share your wins (even the tiny ones), and remind each other to keep going. Having people in your corner makes staying committed and staying on track easier.

Throughout the challenge, keep a journal to record your thoughts and observations. There will be days when it's easy and days when it's not. That's part of the process. But you build something more substantial inside you every day you choose to keep going. By the end, you'll have created more than a habit: you'll have built a practice. You have created a way of loving yourself a little more, one day at a time.

And the best part? Self-love doesn't end on Day 30. This challenge is just the beginning. You can keep these rituals with you, let them grow with you, and return to them whenever you need a reminder of just how deeply you deserve to be loved by *yourself*.

## Your Self-Love Journey: A Lifelong Commitment

Self-love isn't something you master once and then forget–it's a lifelong relationship with yourself, one that deepens and shifts as you grow. Think of it as a journey, not a destination. On some days, it might feel easy and natural. On other days, it might take effort just to be kind to yourself. But like any significant relationship, it's worth showing up for daily. Do you remember imagining self-love as a garden? In some seasons, it will thrive. At other times, it may require more care. Either way, your job is to keep tending to it with patience, compassion, and the willingness to begin again whenever needed.

Making a conscious commitment can help anchor your self-love journey. Try writing a personal self-love pledge or manifesto. It doesn't have to be long, just a few sentences that reflect what you want to promise yourself. For example: "I choose to speak kindly to myself, even when I make mistakes," or "I will honor my needs and celebrate who I am becoming." Tape it to your mirror. Add it to your journal. Let it remind you, especially on the harder days, that you're in this long term. You might also choose to check in with yourself regularly–monthly, seasonally, whenever it feels right. Ask yourself: "What's been working lately? What needs more attention? Where have I shown up for myself?" These quiet moments of reflection help you stay grounded and connected to your growth.

As you continue on this journey, remember that change and evolution are important elements. You'll discover new parts of yourself. Your needs will shift. Your version of self-love will expand, and that's a good thing. Self-reflection is your compass: it keeps you honest with yourself and helps you keep moving forward with intention. Gratitude also plays a decisive role here. When you pause to appreciate how far you've come or what's beautiful in your life right now, you reinforce your inner sense of worth. It's not about being perfect. It's about being present with yourself and being there for yourself.

Loving yourself doesn't mean you'll always feel amazing. It means you keep showing up for yourself, even when it's hard. You don't need to have everything figured out. You just need to keep going–gently, consistently, and with care. Because the more you practice loving yourself, the more you build a life that reflects that love in everything you do.

As you finish this book, know that you're not just turning a page–you're stepping into a stronger, more grounded version of yourself. You've explored your identity, challenged your inner critic, celebrated your strengths, and planted seeds of confidence, mindfulness, and growth. But this is just the beginning. Learning to love yourself is not a one-time lesson; it's a practice you return to again and again. Some days will be easier than others, and that's okay. Keep showing up for yourself. Keep listening to your needs. Continue to be gentle when things feel messy, and take pride in even the smallest steps forward. You are not alone, and you are more than enough. This journey is yours–unique, powerful, and still unfolding. And I'm cheering you on every step of the way.

## Did you do your good deed for the day?

You have almost finished this book, thank you. That means more than I can put into words. If this book supported you in any way, if it helped you feel seen, think differently, or breathe a little easier... Would you take a moment to share that? Make it your good deed of the day and help me out?

Books like this grows because of people like you. Through word of mouth. Through honest words. And your voice truly matters. When you share what this book meant to you, someone else might discover it at exactly the right time. **Your words could be the reason another girl picks up this book and realize she's not alone.** Be the reason she starts her own self-love journey.

So I want to ask you something: What would *you* have wanted someone to say to help you find this book? That's what your review can be. A small light left on for someone who is still finding their way IIt doesn't have to be long. It doesn't have to be perfect. It just has to be yours.

If you do decide to share, thank you. You're not just supporting this book. You're helping someone else feel ready to begin. You're passing on something real. Something kind. Something powerful. Your voice matters. Your story matters. And your words might be the exact ones someone else needs to hear. Thank you for being here. Thank you for being part of this.

With love and gratitude,
Miranda

**If you're open to helping, here's how:**

**Scan the QR code**

**Write what feels true to you**

**Thank you so much**

SCAN ME

@THESELFLOVECOMPASS

# Conclusion

As we come to the end of our journey together, I want to take a moment to reflect on the incredible path we've walked. Throughout this book, we've explored the transformative power of self-love and how it can shape your life as a teen girl. We've talked about embracing your unique identity, nurturing your mind and body, and building resilience in the face of challenges.

Each chapter has been a stepping stone on this path of self-discovery. We've looked at body positivity, the strength found in being vulnerable, and the joy of creative expression. We've explored strategies for managing social pressure, fostering healthy relationships, and cultivating mindfulness. These tools are more than words on a page: they are anchors you can return to repeatedly.

And I want to be honest with you: this journey might not always be easy. Some of the ideas in this book might've felt like, "Yeah, right, as if it's that simple." I get it. I've been there. But I've also done the work and seen how much growth is possible. One day, you'll look back and realize your mindset has shifted. You'll notice how you handle things differently. And that moment, that quiet "woah, I've changed" moment, makes every effort worth it.

As you close this book, I hope you have a renewed confidence and a deeper understanding of your worth. Self-love isn't a destination; it's a lifelong practice. It's about standing up for yourself every day, being kind when things feel messy, and choosing to love who you are right now, not just your future version.

Use the tools from this book as reminders. Let them ground you. Let them lift you when you need it. And come back to these pages when life gets hard, because it most likely will. Let them remind you of what you already know: you are strong, you are enough, and you're never alone.

By choosing self-love as your compass, you're joining a powerful movement. You become part of a ripple effect that inspires other girls to stand taller, speak louder, and love themselves more fiercely. So start the conversations. Share your growth. Be the reason someone else realizes they're not broken; they're just beginning their journey.

As you keep growing, I want to leave you with the words of Michelle Obama: *"You may not always have a comfortable life, and you will not always be able to solve all of the world's problems at once, but don't ever underestimate the importance you can have because history has shown us that courage can be contagious, and hope can take on a life of its own."*

Your courage to love yourself entirely is powerful. It has the potential to change not just your life but the lives of everyone you meet. Let your self-love be a light that guides you and others through anything.

Writing this book has been one of the most personal things I've ever done. Every chapter, every example, and every question was created with you in mind, with the hope that you'd feel seen, supported, and stronger by the time you reached this page. It has been a labor of love for the teenage me who needed this book, for the teenager in our family struggling to find her way, and for you wherever you are on your journey. I didn't write this as someone who has it all figured out but as someone who's been through the hard stuff, asked the same questions you're asking now, and found her way, one imperfect step at a time.

If this book resonated with you, if something helped, or if something felt missing, I would genuinely love to hear from you. If you want to be the first to know about any future courses or projects to do with The Self-Love Compass, or other publications like books, coloring books and journals, do not hesitate to sign up at www.theselflovecompass.com. If you want to have a chat with me, you can reach me at hello@theselflovecompass.com. Don't be a stranger!

If you take just one thing with you from this book, let it be this: you are worthy of love exactly as you are, not just when you've reached some invisible finish line. Self-love is messy, evolving, and brave. I hope this book helped you see that your voice matters, your story matters, and *you* matter.

So, my dear, go forward with courage. Be proud of who you are. Stand in your power. Love yourself deeply, loudly, and without apology. The world needs your voice. This book is just the beginning of your journey, and I am honored to have walked this part with you. Thanks for letting me be part of your journey. I'm so proud of you.

With love and gratitude,

Miranda

# References

-*10 Empowering Crafts for Girls: Boost Confidence Through Creativity*. ( n.d.). https://www.fearlesslygirl.com/blog/10-empowering-crafts-for-girls-boost-confidence-through-creativity-
-*12 Ways to Practice Self Care for Teens - Sedona Sky Academy*. (n.d.). h ttps://www.sedonasky.org/blog/--actice-self-care-for-teens *Body Positivity & Female Empowerment TikTok Creators | The influence agency*. (n.d.). https://theinfluenceagency.com/blog/body-positivity-female-empowerment-tiktok-creators
-*75 Mindfulness Activities for Teens, Worksheets, & Questions*. (n.d.) . https://www.carepatron.com/guides/mindfulness-activities-for-teens
-*A Quote by Lady Gaga*. (n.d.) . https://www.goodreads.com/quotes/222350-you-have-to-be-unique-and-different-and-shine-in
-*A Quote From 13 Things Mentally Strong Women Don't do*. ( n.d.). https://www.goodreads.com/quotes/10684942-be-the-woman-who-fixes-another-woman-s-crown-without-telling
-*A Quote From Becoming*. (n.d.). https://www.goodreads.com/quotes/9582485-friendships-between-women-as-any-woman-will-tell-you-are
-Aacap. (n.d.). *Stress Management and Teens*. https://www.aacap.org/AACAP/Families_and_Youth/Facts_for_Families/FFF-Guide/Helping-Teenagers-With-Stress-066.aspx
-Amy. (2023, March 10). *10 Women Role Models + Ideas for Sparking Kids' Passions*. Lingokids - the Playlearning™ App in English. https://lingokids.com/blog/posts/10-inspiring-female-role-models-for-children
-Blaise. (2022, March 30). *30-Day Self-love Challenge – Love Yourself More*. Dear Self, Grow. https://dearselfgrow.com/30-day-self-love-challenge/
-Briana. (2021, January 6). *Who am I?: Journaling Prompts For Self-Discovery and Self-Reflection*. Learning to Be Free. https://www.learningtobefree.com/2019/07/16/journaling-prompts-for-self-discovery/
-Classroom, C. (2022, December 20). Teaching Self-Compassion to Teenagers: Why It's Important. *Calm Classroom*. https://blog.calmclassroom.com/teaching-self-compas-

sion-teenagers-important
-Davis, H. (2024, February 29). *Fashion as a Catalyst for Teen Self-Expression — CatlinSpeak*. CatlinSpeak.
https://www.catlinspeak.com/speak/fashion-as-a-catalyst-for-teen-self-expression#:~:text=Fashion%20serves%20as%20a%20means,be%20difficult%20to%20articulate%20verbally.
-Desk, L. (2022, November 25). 'If You Are Broken, You Do Not Have to Stay Broken': Selena Gomez. *The Indian Express*. https://indianexpress.com/article/lifestyle/life-positive/if-you-are-broken-you-do-not-have-to-stay-broken-selena-gomez-8276461/
-E. Ackerman, C., & Lancia, G. (2018, February 12). *Cognitive Restructuring Techniques for Reframing Thoughts*. PositivePsychology. https://positivepsychology.com/cbt-cognitive-restructuring-cognitive-distortions/
-E. Ackerman, C., & Nash, J. (2017, November 20). *40 Empathy Activities & Worksheets for Students & Adults*. PositivePsychology. https://positivepsychology.com/kindness-activities-empathy-worksheets/
-*Exploring Mirror Work: A Guide to Self-Healing and Personal Growth - Centre of Excellence*. (n.d.). https://www.centreofexcellence.com/what-is-mirror-work/
-Ferrera, A. (n.d.). *My Identity is a Superpower -- Not an Obstacle* [Video]. TED Talks. https://www.ted.com/talks/america_ferrera_my_identity_is_a_superpower_not_an_obstacle
-Finley, T., & Blay, Z. (2015, September 1). 9 Quotes From Zendaya That Remind us Just How Awesome She Is. *HuffPost*. https://www.huffpost.com/entry/9-quotes-from-zendaya-that-remind-us-just-how-awesome-she-is_n_55e5c1eee4b0b7a9633a3c9c
-Garey, J. (2024, June 5). *13 Ways to Boost Your Daughter's Self-Esteem*. Child Mind Institute. https://childmind.org/article/13-ways-to-boost-your-daughters-self-esteem/
-Ginsburg, K. (2023, March 22). *Building Resilience: The 7 Cs*. Center for Parent and Teen Communication. https://parentandteen.com/building-resilience-in-teens/
-Greenidge, K. (2020, July 15). Yara Shahidi Has Been Preparing for This Moment Since Birth. *ELLE*. https://www.elle.com/culture/celebrities/a33267329/yara-shahidi-interview/
-Hölscher, S. I. E., Schachner, M. K., Juang, L. P., & Altoè, G. (2024). Promoting Adolescents' Heritage Cultural Identity Development: Exploring The Role of Autonomy and Relatedness Satisfaction in School-Based Interventions. *Journal of Youth and Adolescence*, *53*(11), 2460–2479. https://doi.org/10.1007/s10964-024-02017-3
-Houston, E., & Neuhaus, M. (2020, January 30). *21 Self-Determination Skills and Activities to Utilize Today*. Positivepsychology. https://positivepsychology.com/self-determination-skills-activities/
-*How to Help Your Teen Navigate Social Media*. (n.d.). Mayo Clinic.
https://www.mayoclinic.org/healthy-lifestyle/tween-and-teen-health/in-depth/teens-and-social-media-use/art-20474437
-*How to Identify and Manage Your Emotional Triggers*. (2020, November 13). Healthline. https://www.healthline.com/health/mental-health/emotional-triggers
-Inge, C. (2020, October 15). *4 Self Love Myths That Aren't Doing You Any Favors*. Human Design With Christie Inge. https://christieinge.com/self-love-myths/
-Inspirational Quotes From Our Favorite Female Role Models. (2019a, August 29). *Ellevate*. https://www.ellevatenetwork.com/articles/7194-inspirational-quotes-from-our-favorite-female-role-models
-International Women's Day. (n.d.). *52 Inspirational Quotes for Women*

*to Share Throughout the Year*. https://www.internationalwomensday.com/Missions/19614/52-inspirational-quotes-for-women-to-share-throughout-the-year
-Jackson, C. (2024, May 20). *The Power of Positive Affirmations: Boosting Teen Confidence and Mental Health - Positive Presence global*. Positive Presence Global. https://positivepresenceglobal.com/the-power-of-positive-affirmations-boosting-teen-confidence-and-mental-health/
-Jesse. (2024, September 25). *Empowering Teens: The Journey of Expressing Individuality in Adolescence*. theattitudeadvantage.com . https://theattitudeadvantage.com/all-posts/empowering-teens-the-journey-of-expressing-individuality-in-adolescence/
-Krzymowski, J. (2025, January 2). *The Link Between Social Media and Body Image Issues Among Youth in the United States - Ballard Brief*. Ballard Brief. https://ballardbrief.byu.edu/issue-briefs/the-link-between-social-media-and-body-image-issues-among-youth-in-the-united-states
-Lajnef, K. (2023). The Effect of Social Media Influencers' on Teenagers Behavior: An Empirical Study Using Cognitive Map Technique. *Current Psychology*, *42*(22), 19364–19377. https://doi.org/10.1007/s12144-023-04273-1
-Lcsw, M. V. (2025, May 29). *Setting Healthy Boundaries for Teens*. Mental Health Center Kids. https://mentalhealthcenterkids.com/blogs/articles/boundaries-for-teens
-Lpc-S, A. D. (2024, September 30). *Digital Detox for Teens: Why Is It OK to Disconnect*. Clearfork Academy. https://clearforkacademy.com/blog/digital-detox-for-teens/
-McKeown, K. (2025, June 11). *Mindful Social Media for Teens*. Empowering Education. https://empoweringeducation.org/blog/mindful-social-media-for-teens/
-*Mindfulness Exercises (for Teens)*. (n.d.). https://kidshealth.org/en/teens/mindful-exercises.html
-*Opinion | Lizzo: Self-care Is Rooted in Self-preservation, Not Just Mimosas and Spa Days*. (2021, July 2). NBC News. https://www.nbcnews.com/think/opinion/self-care-has-be-rooted-self-preservation-not-just-mimosas-ncna993661
-Rodulfo, K. (2016, August 12). Simone Biles Would Like You to Not Compare Her to Male Athletes. *ELLE*. https://www.elle.com/culture/news/a38468/simone-biles-im-not-the-next-usain-bolt-michael-phelps/
-Room. (2022, August 4). *How to Negotiate With Your Teen*. Spark & Stitch Institute. https://sparkandstitchinstitute.com/how-to-negotiate-with-your-teen/
-Rosa, C., & Leach, S. (2019, January 29). 12 Famous Women Share Failure Quotes on Overcoming Adversity. *Glamour*. https://www.glamour.com/story/famous-women-failure-quotes#:~:text=Anna%20Wintour,grateful%20for%20to%20this%20day.
-Self-Compassion. (2024a, June 21). *Self-Compassion Research by Kristin Neff*. https://self-compassion.org/the-research/
-Self-Compassion. (2024b, November 26). *Self-Compassion Scales | Kristin Neff*. https://self-compassion.org/self-compassion-scales-for-researchers/
-*Self-Discover Activity Ideas for Teens*. (n.d.). Capitol Region: Sponsor a Scholar. https://www.518elevated.org/wp-content/uploads/2022/02/Self-Discovery-Activities-for-Teens.pdf
-Shapiro, M. (2022, August 31). Harnessing the Healing Power of Music. *Johns Hopkins Medicine*. https://www.hopkinsmedicine.org/news/articles/2022/08/harnessing-the-healing-power-of-music
-Shi, J., Tao, Y., Yan, C., Zhao, X., Wu, X., Zhang, T., Zhong, C., Sun, J., & Hu, M. (2023). A Study on the Correlation Between Family Dynamic Factors and Depression in Adolescents. *Frontiers in Psychiatry*, *13*. https://doi.org/10.3389/fpsyt.2022.1025168

-Steenstra, B. (2024, November 15). The Ideal Mindset: 31 Famous Individuals Who Overcame Huge Setbacks. *Becomedamngood*. https://www.becomedamngood.com/post/the-ideal-mindset-14-famous-individuals-who-overcame-huge-setbacks
-*Supporting LGBTQ+ youth*. (2024, November 29). Adolescent and School Health. https://www.cdc.gov/healthy-youth/lgbtq-youth/index.html
-Tao, W., Zhao, D., Yue, H., Horton, I., Tian, X., Xu, Z., & Sun, H. (2022a). The Influence of Growth Mindset on the Mental Health and Life Events of College Students. *Frontiers in Psychology, 13*. https://doi.org/10.3389/fpsyg.2022.821206
-Tao, W., Zhao, D., Yue, H., Horton, I., Tian, X., Xu, Z., & Sun, H. (2022b). The Influence of Growth Mindset on the Mental Health and Life Events of College Students. *Frontiers in Psychology, 13*. https://doi.org/10.3389/fpsyg.2022.821206
-Team, G. (2024, January 18). *11 Tips for a Morning Routine That Supports Mental Health - GoodTherapy.org therapy blog*. GoodTherapy.org Therapy Blog. https://www.goodtherapy.org/blog/11-tips-for-a-morning-routine-that-supports-mental-health-1022197/
-Team, P. (1970, January 21). *50 Empowering Quotes for Women | ProFlowers blog*. ProFlowers Blog. https://www.proflowers.com/blog/empowering-quotes
-Telloian, C. (2021, October 4). *All About Mindful Breathing*. Psych Central. https://psychcentral.com/health/mindful-breathing
-*The Power of Vulnerability Quotes by Brené Brown*. ( n.d.). https://www.goodreads.com/work/quotes/43101666-the-power-of-vulnerability-teachings-on-authenticity-connection-and-c
-*Values Worksheets for Teens | Therapist Aid*. (n.d.-a). Therapist Aid. https://www.therapistaid.com/therapy-worksheets/values/adolescents
-*Values Worksheets for Teens | Therapist Aid*. (n.d.-b). Therapist Aid. https://www.therapistaid.com/therapy-worksheets/values/adolescents
-Wong, D. (2024, April 8). *Communication Skills for Teens: 7 Skills Every Teen Should Develop*. Daniel Wong. https://www.daniel-wong.com/2024/04/08/communication-skills-for-teens/
-Yassin, F. (2024a, April 3). *A Picture Paints a Thousand Words: The Benefits of Arts Therapies for Teen Mental Health*. thewavecl inic.com. https://thewaveclinic.com/blog/a-picture-paints-a-thousand-words-the-benefits-of-arts-therapies-for-teen-mental-health/
-Yassin, F. (2024b, April 3). *A Picture Paints a Thousand Words: The Benefits of Arts Therapies for Teen Mental Health*. thewavecl inic.com. https://thewaveclinic.com/blog/a-picture-paints-a-thousand-words-the-benefits-of-arts-therapies-for-teen-mental-health/
-York, C. C. O. N. (n.d.). *Media Literacy for Students in a Digital Age | Citizenship | Carnegie Corporation of New York*. Carnegie Corporation of New York. https://www.carnegie.org/our-work/article/media-literacy-for-students-in-a-digital-age/
-Yourtherapysource. (2022, September 14). *SMART GOALS FOR TEENS - Your Therapy Source*. Your Therapy Source. https://www.yourtherapysource.com/blog1/2022/08/11/smart-goals-for-teens-3/
-Yousafzai, M. (2022, April 11). Malala Yousafzai: Nobel Peace Prize Acceptance Speech. *Malala Fund*. https://malala.org/newsroom/malala-nobel-speech

Printed in Dunstable, United Kingdom

79898876R00077